Preventing
Adolescent Abuse

———

Preventing Adolescent Abuse

Effective Intervention Strategies and Techniques

BY

Richard P. Barth
University of California, Berkeley

AND

David S. Derezotes
University of Utah

Lexington Books

D.C. Heath and Company/Lexington, Massachusetts/Toronto

Library of Congress Cataloging-in-Publication Data
Barth, Richard P., 1952-
　　Preventing adolescent abuse : effective intervention strategies
　and techniques / by Richard P. Barth and David S. Derezotes.
　　　p.　　cm.
　　Includes bibliographical references.
　　ISBN 0-669-20903-1 (alk. paper)
　　1. Social work with teenagers—United States.　2. Teenagers-
　-United States—Abuse of—Prevention.　　I. Derezotes, David S.
　II. Title
　HV1431.B37　1990
　362.7'67'0835—dc20　　　　　　　　　　　　　　　90-30978
　　　　　　　　　　　　　　　　　　　　　　　　　　CIP

Published simultaneously in Canada
Printed in the United States of America
Casebound International Standard Book Number: 0-669-20903-1
Library of Congress Catalog Card Number: 90-30978

The paper used in this publication meets
the minimum requirements of American National Standard
for Information Sciences—Permanence of Paper
for Printed Library Materials, ANSI Z39.48-1984.

Year and number of this printing:

90 91 92 8 7 6 5 4 3 2 1

With the deepest gratitude to Paul and Gary who gave so much counsel and support and so little grief to their little brother. (R.P.B.)

To those adolescents who were not protected from abuse, that their stories teach us how to better protect others. (D.D.)

Contents

Figures and Tables

Preface and Acknowledgments

Adolescence is a time of great vulnerability. Parents and service providers may understand its jeopardy even more keenly than adolescents, but all parties involved know that every day includes sundry risks of harm. Interpersonal relationships—whether parent to adolescent or peer to peer—are often confusing and sometimes get beyond control. Service providers suffer the same confused relationships to adolescents and often don't know what to do to reach these young adults. With a few exceptions, adolescent services have sharply diminished in the last few years because society appears to have concluded that adolescents are able to manage without significant social services. The personal vulnerability of adolescence is compounded by the cultural and institutional neglect of their needs. Adolescents suffer abuse at rates similar to other childhood age groups but they are less likely to receive formal services.

Prevention is a course that has not been abandoned for adolescents, and, if anything, our schools now offer a larger array of life skills courses than ever before. Society, and the school's that are responsible to translate its culture, increasingly recognizes that physically and sexually abused, drug-using, pregnant, hungry, angry, and suicidal students thwart the best efforts of educators to create able citizens. Longstanding life skills classes in cooking, sewing, drivers education, and sexuality education have new content that includes child abuse prevention. High school child abuse prevention programs are beginning to penetrate America's schools, although they are different from prior family-life and life-skills education programs insofar as they are typically delivered by community-based child abuse prevention agencies that visit the schools to deliver their message. To date, there is no published analysis of these programs.

This book arises from the first project to describe and analyze high school child abuse prevention programs. The authors received two years of support from the State of California Office of Child Abuse Prevention to study the state's high school child abuse prevention program. This is the most far reaching high school child abuse prevention program that exists today, and reaches roughly 350,000 adolescents each year. We came to the project with the benefits of experience as parents, social workers with abused and abusing adolescents and child abuse victims, parent-educators and psychotherapists with abusive parents, authors and implementers of life skills training programs, and evaluators of prevention programs in other areas. We were also colleagues of a team of researchers, led by Neil Gilbert and Jill Duerr Berrick, who were a step ahead of us in evaluating the state's preschool and elementary school child abuse prevention programs. Working in their wake left rough waters at times, but it also provided us with a clearer image of the evaluation and sociopolitical waterscape.

Partly as a result, we developed an evaluation process that involved considerable give and take between program providers, evaluators, and Office of Child Abuse Prevention staff. All parties participated in instrumental development. As soon as we had preliminary findings we distributed them to all programs under evaluation and convened a large group of interested parties for a dialogue meetings to discuss our findings and preliminary recommendations. The recommendations were heatedly debated and discussed and later modified. We subsequently hel¹ a workshop at the annual statewide child abuse conference and encouraged additional commentary from our audience. Yet another round of commentary was received from Office of Child Abuse Prevention staff when we submitted our revised executive summary. Presentations of our findings at the eighth National Conference on Child Abuse in Neglect in Salt Lake City in October 1989 and at the Western Regional Conference of the Child Welfare League of America in Phoenix in November 1989 further clarified our thinking. All in all, we created numerous opportunities to test the findings and conclusions presented in these pages. This book goes well beyond the report of our evaluation, however, and presents a grander framework for understanding and redirecting adolescent abuse prevention programs.

We have written this book to appeal to lay child abuse prevention specialists, social workers, counselors, psychologists, and other readers interested in child abuse prevention programs and evaluation. The first chapter offers a research base for understanding adolescent abuse—its incidence and social and familial roots. We consider ways that adolescents are victims and perpetrators of abuse. The second chapter reviews the research on child abuse prevention programs and also draws on lessons from allied (e.g., smoking and drugs) life skills training programs with adolescents. The third and fourth chapters describe the methods and outcomes of studies of California and national approaches to adolescent child abuse prevention. Chapters 5 and 6 consider the implications of the research for a K–12 child abuse prevention curriculum and propose a more theoretically sound, ambitious, and efficient strategy for the delivery of adolescent child abuse prevention services.

We have grappled with many difficult issues in preparing this book, and one of the earliest and thorniest was what to call the phenomenon that the programs we are evaluating seek to prevent. *Adolescent maltreatment* is a term that covers the range of assaults on an adolescent's well-being and has the considerable virtue of giving no more emphasis to physical and sexual abuse than to psychological and physical neglect. On the other hand, *child abuse* or *adolescent abuse* are far more often used and understood terms in the public domain, and services delivered to prevent adolescent maltreatment are typically funded by offices of *child abuse* and delivered by *child abuse* agencies. Primarily for this reason, we have chosen to use *child abuse* throughout the book. The reader should have no doubt, however, that we use this term to refer to the entire range of abuse. We struggled with a somewhat similar problem in considering whether to use the term *acquaintance rape* or *acquaintance assault* to describe the topic of adolescent prevention programs. Certainly, we recognize the difference between rape and assault, and the data tells us that rape is much less frequent than assault between adolescents. Using the term *acquaintance assault* has the virtue of signaling the intent of programs and of our recommendations—that is, to reduce the whole spectrum of sexually related ways (not just the most serious ways) that adolescents victimize each other. On the other hand, the convention of using *acquaintance rape* is strong and many programs define it to be synonymous with *acquaintance assault*. We have chosen to use *acquaintance rape* as the all-inclusive term unless we otherwise specify.

Child abuse is a relatively new field. Twenty years ago there were no programs specifically designated to prevent child abuse. In contrast, the public educational system and family and child welfare agencies have been concerned about children's welfare since the mid-1800s. We have endeavored to bridge these three fields in our work. This is not always an easy or a popular endeavor. Our experience working with child abuse prevention providers tells us that these are dedicated, energized, people who interact in ways that are very personal and antibureaucratic; going to a child abuse prevention conference is likely to yield many laughs, a few tears, and an inner buzz reminiscent of participation in the human potential and peace movements of the 1960s and 1970s. In comparison, few cry or sing at education or child welfare meetings. In short, these are unique organizations with equally unique staffs and ethos. The ideal that we propose in various forms in our final chapters is to enlist the strengths, stability, and training of the education and child welfare systems and, at the same time, engage the energy, expertise, and talent of child abuse prevention specialists in helping develop more comprehensive child abuse prevention programs.

A book of this size requires teamwork and we had wonderful teammates in this enterprise. The authors are indebted to the students, parents, professionals, Child Abuse Prevention Training Act (CAPTA) providers and administrators, and State of California Office of Child Abuse Prevention (OCAP) staff who shared their experiences with us. Our OCAP project monitors—Linda Reese, Aurora Dominguez, Ingrid Petty, Maria Giotes, and Rose Munsey, along with Beth Hardesty Fife, Bob Green, and Rhoda Katz—provided us with valuable information and support. Sherri

Patterson, Mary Beth Roden, Michael Spokane, Myrtis Stout, Pnina Tobin, Kay Wallis, and staff from the training centers provided helpful suggestions on the content and form of items in our questionnaire. We particularly want to thank those many CAPTA providers who were able to keep a receptive and open mind to this research process and who always seemed willing to examine their assumptions, goals, and teaching strategies. Lin Wan I, Cassandra Coe, Jack Light, Danielle Sherman, Holly Danforth Vugia, Robert Adwere-Boamoh, Bonnie Bhatti, Marcia Meyers, and Claudia Waters provided a range of invaluable research services. Wendy Goss, Sharon Ikami, and Susan Katzenellenbogen prepared this book with great skill and patience. Jill Duerr Berrick and Neil Gilbert read earlier drafts and provided useful suggestions. The intent to find efficient and effective ways to protect our youth from child abuse is shared by many; responsibility for the conclusions and recommendations in this report is ours alone. Funding for the study was provided by the State of California, Department of Social Services, Office of Child Abuse Prevention Grant #C7101.

Heartfelt thanks for help with this project must include Harry Specht, Dean of the School of Social Welfare, for providing much scholarly and personal support to us both. I (R.B.) reserve my greatest appreciation for my wife, Nancy Dickinson, and my children, James and Catrina, who have so willingly accepted my wish to spend my Tuesday nights writing: this is what I was writing. They all inspire me to try to analyze services in a way that leads to a safer world. I (D.D.) thank my best friend, Diane Drost (who also happens to be my wife), who supported my efforts to complete this research project, as well as my son, Nathan, for whom I wish not only an abuse-free, but a wonderfull and growth-full adolescence.

1
Incidence and Circumstances

The abuse of adolescents in their high school years is a serious problem. Approximately 1.7 million cases of child maltreatment are reported annually in the United States with 24 percent involving youth between twelve and seventeen years old (The American Humane Association 1986). Adolescents are abused in approximate proportion to their numbers in the population of all young people (Finkelhor 1986; Garbarino, Schellenbach, and Sebes 1986; Schillenbach and Guerney 1987). The National Incidence Study (NIS) indicates that sexual and emotional abuse reports on adolescents are more prevalent than neglect or physical abuse reports (National Center on Child Abuse and Neglect (NCCAN) 1981). Physical abuse of adolescents is as common as it is for younger children. Sexual abuse of adolescents is more common (Eckenrode et al 1988). Neglect is less often reported for adolescents. In the NIS sample, adolescent female victims are twice as common as males (Olson & Holmes, 1983).

State and local reports on adolescent abuse complement national studies, and often show adolescents as receiving disproportionately low levels of reports. Child abuse reports in Illinois between 1981 and 1984 indicate that children fourteen to seventeen years represented from 11.8 to 12.8 percent of the reports; considerably lower than for any other age grouping (Testa and Lawlor 1985). (Among sexual abuse reports, however, fourteen to seventeen year olds represented 25 percent of the total.) New York state data from the same period indicates that reports of child abuse of youth fifteen and over are about thirteen percent of the total (New York State Council on Children and Families

1988). Only a study of adolescent abuse in Minnesota, in which 42 percent of all confirmed cases of child abuse occurred against persons 12 to 17, exceeds the national abuse rate of 24 percent (Blum and Runyan 1980). Almost three- of five females reported sexual abuse, whereas only 16 percent of the male victims so reported. Bruises, cuts, and welts were the most common findings in male adolescent abuse, accounting for 70 percent of reports. For females, these reports accounted for 41 percent of reports.

For the most part, research describes the age of most sexual abuse victims as well below adolescence. Early adolescence may be the most likely time for females to be abused, although males are more likely to be abused as children. In their surveys of college students, Finkelhor (1979) and Haugaard (1987) found the mean age of girls at the time of sexual assault to be ten and the mean age for boys to be eleven and ten, respectively. Sedney and Brooks (1984) found the median age of sexual assault onset for girls to be nine. Wyatt (1985) reports that abuse occurred for white girls between six and eight years of age and for black girls from nine to twelve. Pierce and Pierce (1984) also found that black children were abused younger—on the average at about eight years of age—than white children who averaged about ten years old at the time of the sexual abuse.

High school youth do not often report child abuse. When they do they are most often female. The incidence of adolescent abuse reports for females peaked during middle adolescence (fourteen to fifteen years old) in Minnesota (Blum and Runyan 1980). Reports of sexual abuse cases of females have bimodal peaks at about age four and fifteen (Powers and Eckenrode 1988). In Wexler's (1989) clinical sample, just 13 percent of abused children were age fifteen to eighteen. Hampton and Newberger (1985) studied child abuse reports (from hospitals) of incidents resulting in injury and found that sexual abuse in the thirteen- to seventeen-year-old group represented only 16 percent of the reports. Sexual abuse was most often reported from the hospital to social services (81 percent) in contrast to physical neglect (66 percent) and physical abuse (76 percent) or emotional abuse (36 percent). The thirteen- to seventeen-year-old group represented only 16 percent of the reports.

Although these data square with our experience, readers should note that adolescent abuse statistics are collected in different ways from place to place and time to time and should not garner much confidence. Most often the age of abuse victims is not reported in statistical summaries, making the incidence of adolescent abuse still harder to determine. Also, abused adolescents are underserved, so the gap between the incidence and reports of abuse is probably quite wide for this group. Adolescent boys are less likely to be reported as victims of all forms of abuse and less likely to have their cases substantiated, despite the probability that they are physically abused more often than girls (Rosenthal 1988). Wexler (1989) found that among the victims of sexual abuse ages fifteen or older, 77 percent had disclosed their abuse themselves. In all other age groups, victims were only about equally likely to disclose their victimization as have it reported by others. Consistent with their being left to their own devices to get help, adolescents least often receive crisis services. The extent to which underreporting influences our estimate of the incidence of physical abuse, sexual abuse, neglect, and psychological maltreatment in adolescence is unknown.

Not only are adolescents at risk to become victims of maltreatment, but adolescents abuse or will abuse peers and younger children. An estimated one-third of all sex offenders who molest children are adolescents (Beth Lennon, personal communication, October 1987). In Russell's (1986) study almost one-quarter of abusers of females were adolescents, and as many as 50 percent of boys who are molested may be molested by adolescents (Gail Ryan, personal communication, October 1989). The National Center on Child Abuse and Neglect's (1986) report covering 1976 to 1981 indicates a striking increase of documented cases nationwide, from six thousand in 1976 to one hundred thousand in 1984. The FBI indicates that 30 percent of the reported rape arrests in the United States during 1980 were made on adolescents (U.S. Department of Justice 1983). Their victims are most often adolescents. Table 1–1 provides a comparison of the number of male and female adolescent sexual assaults reported by age grouping in the years 1975 and 1985. Younger youth are increasingly arrested, although assaults by high school age adolescents are most common. Groth (1978) estimates that an addi-

Table 1–1
U.S. Sexual Assaults, Age-Specific Arrests: 1975 to 1985[1]

	1975 Rate	1975 Percent	1985 Rate	1985 Percent	Change in Rate (in percent)
12 yrs. old and younger					
Male	5.7	1	11.3	1	98.2
Female	.7	*	1.4	*	100.0
13 to 14 yrs. old					
Male	69.4	10	133.0	16	91.6
Female	9.3	1	11.8	1	26.9
15 yrs. old					
Male	112.9	18	160.2	19	41.9
Female	18.5	3	14.0	2	− 24.3
16 yrs. old					
Male	127.9	20	146.9	18	15.7
Female	15.6	2	12.9	2	− 17.3
17 yrs. old					
Male	127.0	20	154.7	19	21.0
Female	12.0	2	12.5	2	4.2
18 yrs. old					
Male	129.3	20	155.6	19	20.3
Female	11.2	2	16.2	2	44.6
TOTALS (Averaged)					
Male	95.4	90[2]	127.0	92[2]	33.1
Female	11.2	10	11.5	8	2.4
Combined	106.6	100	138.5	100	35.5

Source: U.S. Department of Justice, Washington, D.C., 1986.
[1]All rates are per 100,000.
[2]Percentage of total, combined rate.
*Indicates less than 1 percent.

tional 5 percent of juvenile sex offenses are committed by *pre*adolescent boys. Although girls have been reported as sex offenders, an estimated 90 percent of reported adolescent offenders are male. The number of adolescent females who commit sex offenses may have been underreported (Groth 1978; Plummer 1981), perhaps because their behavior is likely to be less assaultive than that of boys (Barnard, Fuller, Robbins, and Shaw 1989). Because adolescents are assaultive and assaulted, related prevention programs face a dual challenge.

√ Among all children, abuse is far more likely to be perpetrated by family members against family members than by extra-familial adults against adolescents, but this is probably reversed for adolescents. Across the ages, roughly 30 to 60 percent of sexual abuse is thought to be perpetrated by family members or persons in a familylike role (Haugaard 1987; Russell 1984; Waterman and Lusk 1986), and about 10 percent is perpetrated by strangers (Conte and Berliner 1981; Haugaard 1987; Russell 1986)—the remaining 30 to 60 percent is perpetrated by acquaintances. A higher percentage of acquaintance assault almost certainly occurs among adolescents, although current data collection does not readily allow contrasts among familial, acquaintance, and extrafamilial stranger assaults.

Intrafamilial Adolescent Abuse

We know rather little about the incidence of different types of intrafamilial adolescent abuse. Intrafamilial adolescent physical abuse has traditionally been conceived of as having tripartite origins: (1) families that escalated from harsh disciplining of children to abusive disciplining of adolescents; (2) families that functioned normally until becoming unraveled by the transition to adolescence (Lourie 1979); and (3) families that continue an abusive pattern established in childhood into adolescence. Lourie (1977) and Libbey and Bybee (1979) indicate that between 80 and 90 percent of physical abuse of adolescents begins in adolescence, whereas Garbarino and Gilliam (1980) and Pelcovits et al. (1984) report that roughly half of adolescent abuse cases begin in adolescence. Berdie et al. (1983) and Farber and Joseph (1985) suggest that only 25 percent have adolescent onset and that abuse of adolescents typically began five years earlier.

Although abuse originates under many influences, the developmental literature clearly favors the third model for the origin of abuse. The literature on human development within a family context would suggest that adolescent abuse is more often a lasting experience from childhood. The developmental process is more incremental than abrupt, more even than uneven (Brim and Kagan 1980; Patterson, Dishion, and Bank 1984).

Sexual abuse may differ from physical abuse, neglect, and emotional maltreatment in its continuity, as single occurrences constitute most of the sexual abuse cases in every major study. The rates of one-time occurrences range from 58 percent in Sedney and Brooks's (1984) sample to 93 percent in the Canadian Probability Sample (Badgley et al. 1984). A relatively small percentage of cases—roughly 14 percent—continued for more than one year. Most often the sexual activity was nongenital or genital fondling (from 36 to 52 percent), with cases involving intercourse representing about 5 percent.

Extrafamilial Adolescent Abuse

This conventional tripartite classification of adolescent abuse fundamentally covers the patterns of intrafamilial abuse but requires the addition of two categories for extrafamilial abuse, namely: (4) continuous relationships with peers that involve one or more physical or sexual assaults and (5) encounters with acquaintances or strangers who commit an assault. Thus, programs to prevent adolescent abuse must address a phenomenon that varies in origins, longevity, and form in ways that we do not clearly understand.

Extrafamilial abuse of adolescents most often involves peer acquaintances. As adolescents start to socially interact more with the opposite sex, they are also exposed to a greater risk of acquaintance assault and rape. Acquaintance rape is a form of adolescent abuse, and is a key concern of many adolescent maltreatment prevention programs. A small but growing body of literature describes a theoretical basis for acquaintance rape prevention programs. However, little consensus exists in many areas of research. Even the definition of acquaintance rape is unclear. Hughes and Sandler (1987) use the narrow, traditional definition of "forced unwanted intercourse with a person you know." Child abuse prevention practitioners tend to use the broader definition in which acquaintance rape includes all forced and unwanted sexual advances from a person one knows. Because the differences between these definitions suggest differences in interpretation, we will attempt to distinguish them. As previously discussed, we will use the term *acquaintance rape* in its broadest sense when discussing forced or unwanted intercourse as well as other forced or unwanted sexual contact. We will reserve *acquaintance assault* for discussing situations that explicitly preclude rape. *Acquaintance rape* data refer to all types of acquaintance assault unless we otherwise specify.

Acquaintance rape is a significant problem for adolescents. Although, the incidence is unknown, the risk for high school students appears high. Most acquaintance rape data are collected on college students. Between 13 and 25 percent of college women report being raped by their peers, and between 6 and 8 percent of college men admit they tried raping college women (Aizenman and Kelley 1988; Hughes and Sandler 1987; Koss and Oros 1982). Of those women who reported being raped, only 57 percent actually called it rape; few of the men who raped or tried to rape women reportedly saw themselves as rapists. Muehlenhard and Linton (1987) report that 77.6 percent of college women and 57.3 percent of college men are involved in sexual aggressions with partners; 14.7 percent of women and 7.1 percent of men have unwanted intercourse. Adolescent sexual assault closely parallels assault by adults in that the vast majority of offenders know their victims—about 85 percent by Ageton's (1983) account. Nelson and Clark's (1986) review concludes that 40 to 60 percent of female sexual assault victims know the offenders personally; Hughes and Sandler (1987) give a figure of 92 percent. In nearly two-thirds of the cases, the offender and the victim were involved in a long-term relationship. Most often the assault followed verbal persuasion or attempts to inebriate the woman. The threat and use of violence occurred in approximately 20 percent of the cases. Overall, 20 percent of all forcible rapes are committed by adolescents (Sourcebook of Criminal Justice Statistics, 1988).

Child molesting behavior often begins in early adolescence (Becker, Cunningham-Rathner, and Kaplan 1986). The majority of adult sex offenders began committing sex offenses in adolescence (Downer 1985). Longo and McFadin (1981) studied forty-three adult sexual offenders and forty-one adolescent offenders and concluded that rapists and child molesters have histories of early exhibitionism and voyeurism. Longo and Groth (1983) note that adult sex offenders frequently came to the attention of a clinician while they were adolescents for inappropriate juvenile sexual behavior, the significance of which was dismissed.

In addition, adolescents molest their siblings: the incidence of sibling abuse in Diana Russell's (1983) sample is 16 percent. Although sibling incest may be less common than sexual assault of nonfamily members, it may well be the most frequently occurring incestuous relationship (Randazzo 1989). A variety of researchers have found rates of incestuous victimization by brothers to be roughly five times that of victimization by fathers (Finkelhor 1979; De Young 1982; Loredo 1982). Sibling incest represents a small percentage of reported intrafamilial sexual abuse, as many cases may go undetected and unreported.

Adolescents also are at risk to commit other forms of abuse. They sometimes baby-sit and find themselves in positions of having to discipline, bathe, and care for younger children. Perhaps the most common setting for a molest committed by an adolescent is when the adolescent is baby-sitting (Barnard et al. 1989). An unknown number of adolescents, perhaps substantial, are physically and psychologically abusive with their peers or with younger children. Most adolescents will eventually become spouses and parents. Some are already parents and will, therefore, eventually come into increased contact with dependent people who are relatively vulnerable to maltreatment.

The Social Ecology of Adolescent Abuse

A social ecology explanation of abuse rings true to an increasingly large group of child abuse scholars and providers. First applied to human development by Urie Bronfenbrenner (1977), the biology-based concept proposes that an individual's environment requires adaptation from individuals residing within. Further, the environment is composed of a series of settings from the family to neighborhood to the political economy and state. The appeal of the concept is its escape from intrapersonal and intrafamilial explanations of child abuse. Jim Garbarino has been the foremost investigator of the link between the social ecology and child abuse, showing in several studies the power of the social environment to predict levels of child abuse (Garbarino 1976; Garbarino and Sherman 1980). He writes, "What then is the special contribution of an ecological perspective? I think it is first and foremost an appreciation of **place**" (emphasis in original) (Garbarino 1981, p. 229). "Neighborhood is typically the ecological niche in which families operate and neighborhoods are one of the principal **places** where one finds the conditions of life that conspire to compound rather than counteract the deficiencies and vulnerabilities of parents" (p. 234). When we think of places we tend to think of areas that have people with similar rather than different incomes, occupations, cultural styles, and educational and community resources. Within places, people do, of course, behave differently. An ecological model also accounts for the social and familial conditions that allow and foster abuse of adolescents because these are also associated with place. Single-parent families, families affected by drugs, families that move often, large families, and families troubled by unemployment often reside in common neighborhoods. Not only these, but certainly these are places where family violence and adolescent abuse are common.

Intrafamilial Abuse

Although abuse occurs across places and family types, it is unevenly distributed across places and populations. That is, like drug abuse, child abuse is found in many places but concentrated in a few. Physical abuse and neglect have long been understood to occur disproportionately among more distressed economic groups (Gil 1970; Pelton 1978). The same may not be true for sexual abuse (Finkelhor 1984; Wyatt 1985). Although it would appear more equitable if otherwise, overall, "the strong association between poverty and abuse is not simply an artifact of the reporting system" (Westat Associates 1981, p. 20); 66 percent of adolescent abuse cases had family incomes below $15,000. Because race and income are associated, black children are disproportionately abused. A full 41 percent of the black families and 25 percent of white families of sexually abused children in Pierce and Pierce's (1984) study were receiving Aid to Families of Dependent Children (AFDC). Numerous investigators have also shown ethnic differences in child abuse and sexual abuse with blacks overrepresented in both (e.g., Lindholm and Willey 1986; Pierce and Pierce 1984; Spearly and Lauderdale 1983). Less clear are other underlying factors that may contribute these tendencies; for example, to what extent are single-mother households, anger about racism, or emersion in a drug-plagued community associated with higher rates of abuse?

Budin and Johnson (1989) indicate that sexual abuse victims were passive, troubled, lonely children from broken homes. Stepparents and paramours are overrepresented in most kinds of abuse. This holds true for adolescents. Stepparents were implicated in between 25 and 40 percent of reporters in the key studies of adolescent abuse (Berdie et al. 1983; Farber and Joseph 1985; Libbee and Bybee 1979; Olson and Holmes 1983) even though only 12 to 15 percent of children live with stepparents. This does not account for abuse by paramours who are overrepresented in the fatal abuse of children and may also be exceptionally prone toward adolescent abuse.

Deisher, Wenet, Papenny, Clark, and Fehrenbach (1982) found that parents and children are isolated, witnessed a lack of parental supervision, and that father incapacitation (from death, imprisonment, or drugs) was often present. Almost half of sibling incest aggressors witnessed one or more sexual acts between parents or a parent and a paramour (Smith and Israel 1987).

National Incidence Study data suggest that social class is not as large a factor in adolescent abuse as it is in child abuse (Westat Associates 1981). A full 85 percent of those reported in Hampton and Newberger (1985) were families with incomes less than $15,000. This is consistent with Garbarino and Gilliam (1980) and Berdie et al. (1983). The NIS also indicates that parental education of abused adolescents is higher than for abused children. Still, poor adolescents are more likely to be victims of abuse than their nonpoor counterparts. Whereas the data is less than perfect, the evidence is clearly on the side of arguing that all children are not equally at risk of harm from child abuse.

Child abuse is associated with social class for many reasons, particularly the lack of information and skills for obtaining agency resources (Giovannoni and Billingsley 1970); lack of resources that temper stress (Spearly and Lauderdale 1983); and greater use of drugs and alcohol, which disinhibit family violence (Lehman and Krupp 1984) and sexual abuse (Pierce and Pierce 1984). The argument that all types of child abuse are class and culturally-linked is not new (Pelton 1978), nor is it an argument that all child abuse is associated with. More to the point, families and children suffering the most social strain are also most likely to suffer adolescent abuse. Efforts to prevent adolescent abuse must address that fact.

Families from the same socioeconomic and ethnic groups tend to dwell in close proximity. Cotterril (1988) argues that the geographic plotting of cases on a map is an important contributor to identifying families at risk. He identified an inner borough of London with double the national average rate of child abuse. Among twenty-three electoral wards with 20,550 households with children under age sixteen, 73 percent of abuse cases were in just sixteen target areas with an average of only 14 households per area! That is, 146 households were the setting for considerably more child abuse than the other twenty thousand. None of the areas was larger than one-half mile across. Eight of those areas contained 50 percent of all the cases in the borough and were stable across the two years of the study. Based on previous work (Garbarino 1976; Garbarino and Crouter 1978), five economic (percent of incomes less than $8,000 and greater than $15,000) and social (percent of female-headed households, percent of married mothers with young children in the labor force, and percent of less-than-one-year residents) indicators were used to predict child abuse rates in local areas (Garbarino and Sherman 1980). These indicators explained about 80 percent of the variance of child abuse among the neighborhoods. From there Cotterril chose two areas that were "outliers" and did not conform to the prediction model: one had a much higher abuse rate and one was much lower than expected. This identification generated further understanding of service needs. A short form to screen neighborhoods for exceptional child abuse risk is provided in Cotterril (1988).

Spearly and Lauderdale (1983) examined 246 Texas counties and also found support for a social ecological model for child abuse reports: the greater the proportions of single mothers and working mothers with very young children and the less the proportion of annual incomes above $15,000 the higher the child abuse report rates. Greater urbanization and fewer county services were also linked with abuse reports. Although the research does not identify the age of the victims, the general literature suggests that adolescent abuse is more similar than different from other kinds of abuse. There is a strong likelihood that adolescent abuse would be frequent in these target areas. The social ecology of sibling incest sounds painfully familiar.

Taken together, these studies and our front line experiences with our most troubled families suggest that

> risk is increasingly concentrated among multi-problem families, families less easily reached by the "easy" and "cheap" methods that responded to the first wave of prevention initiatives. We might observe a similar effect with regard to sexual abuse prevention programs aimed at children. It's easy to reach many children, but as we succeed, risk becomes ever more concentrated among children who already live in multi-problem families (Garbarino 1988, p. 12).

Oddly, although child abuse prevention researchers identify ecological indicators of child abuse risk, prevention service providers deliver universal prevention programs that assume abuse happens in equal measure in all places and parts of society.

An ecological model is stronger than an intergenerational model but they are not entirely separable. Support for the intergenerational transmission of child abuse is generally weak and depends principally on the intergenerational continuity of social stress. That is, if parents continue to live in the stressful environments in which they were reared, they will be likely to continue to be vulnerable to involvement in abuse. Widom's (1989) prospective cohort study of children who were abused and entered the dependency system in the late 1960s found no intergenerational continuity, but he did find that abused children were somewhat more likely to have criminal records as young adults. Although not definitive, this study supports several other analyses (e.g., Jayaratne 1977), which suggest the foolishness of a unilateral prediction that a childhood experience of abuse will have a simple outcome. Kaufman and Zigler's (1987) review concludes that the best estimate of the rate of intergenerational transmission appears to be between 25 and 35 percent. Similarly, Finkelhor (1988) has estimated that not more than 5 percent of male victims of sexual molestation will later in life themselves molest a child, exposing a common misconception of intergenerational continuity that is perpetuated in many child abuse prevention and treatment programs. Although this far exceeds the base rate for abuse in the general population (approximately 5 percent) it suggests that the mediating influences of social environments are much more important than historic factors.

Assaults by Adolescents

The etiology of acquaintance assault and rape is even less certain than its incidence. The social ecology of acquaintance rape is probably quite similar to that of other forms of abuse. As Apter and Propper (1986) indicate, an ecological perspective on youth violence most ably explains the occurrence. Other evidence (U.S. Department of Justice 1986) indicates that juvenile murder, rape, robbery, and aggravated assault have similarly situated victims and perpetrators. Boys and adolescent males who assault siblings and peers often experience troubled home lives, have poor social skills, and experience aggression, dominance, and intimidation (Davis and Leitenberg 1987; Deisher et al 1982).

Although the social ecology of adolescent offenders is currently not well documented (Finkelhor, 1986), the evidence that sexual assault and adolescent violence are reasonably explained by an ecological model strongly suggests a parallel conclusion about adolescent sexual assault.

Geography is, of course, not enough to explain intrafamilial or extrafamilial assault. A more comprehensive model must also include, at minimum, psychological characteristics of the perpetrator (e.g., character disorders, unsocialized rage) and family processes (e.g., parent-adolescent distrust, high spousal conflict). Although knowledge of these characteristics have utility in *treatment*, we argue that they are not particularly useful in the service of *prevention*. We also believe that of all the characteristics of a child abuse model, the social environment is most central and that other psychological and family processes are likely to be overrepresented in families living in troubled areas.

There are behavioral risk factors as well. Muehlenhard and Linton (1987) describe risk factors for acquaintance rape of college-age women: the male initiating and paying for the date; miscommunications about sex, drug, and alcohol use; parking; traditional sex roles; interpersonal violence or adversarial attitudes; and rape myths. In another study of college-age partners (Muehlenhard, Friedman, and Thomas 1985), other risk factors were reported: dates at the man's apartment, the female asked the male out, and the man's traditional attitudes toward women. These findings may also hold for adolescents, although confirmatory research is necessary.

Adolescent abuse arises for many reasons and in families of all types. As reviewed earlier, programs designed to prevent abuse of and by adolescents face the challenge of preventing at least five kinds of phenomenon: (1) impulsive and atypical familial assaults; (2) familial assaults that gradually escalate; (3) familial assaults that are part of a chronic and lasting pattern of caretakers and/or sibling abuse; (4) assaults of and by familiar peers; and (5) assaults of and by strangers and brief acquaintances. Taken separately, these five types of adolescent abuse—which could easily be expanded to seven or eight—call for a like number of intervention programs. Addressing commonalities among them apparently deserves consideration. Indeed, the nature of adolescent maltreatment itself may call for a viewpoint that emphasizes commonality among all forms of abuse of vulnerable people. Adolescent abuse has been characterized as a "bridge" between child abuse, spouse and elder abuse (Garbarino, Schellenbach, and Sebes 1986).

The commonalities that program designers choose will vary, of course, depending on service providers' understanding of adolescent abuse. If program designers believe that adolescent abuse is undergirded by knowledge and attitudes accepting of violence they will design information programs. If they believe in a situational model of assault, they might design a program that teaches adolescents additional skills for avoiding or escaping situations with a high risk of assault. If they believe, as we do, that an ecological model best explains adolescent assault, they will design programs tailored to high-risk areas and families and programs that endeavor to create safer settings for adolescents.

2
Child Abuse and Allied Prevention Efforts

Child Abuse Prevention Programs

Child abuse prevention efforts with adolescents are generally less than a decade old. Although social service agencies have intervened to protect children for more than one hundred years (Gordon 1988), public concern about child abuse reemerged in the 1950s and 1960s along with concerns for civil rights, social responsibility, and equality (Nelson 1985). The first school-based programs with child abuse prevention as their major component did not appear until after 1974 and were scattered throughout the country. Nationally, and in California, school-based sexual abuse prevention programs were initially funded by criminal justice and community-based prevention funds. In recent years, children's trust funds have increasingly supported school-based child abuse prevention programs. As of 1989, forty-three states have children's trust funds, which fund many child abuse prevention programs in America's schools.

The passage of California's AB 2443, the Child Abuse Prevention and Training Act (CAPTA) in 1984, created the most far-reaching, extensive, and ambitious school-based child abuse prevention program in the country (Daro, 1988). Designed to protect children from preschool age through high school by teaching them about abuse, the program is administered by the state's Office of Child Abuse Prevention (OCAP) and allocates $10.1 million per year toward that end. About $9.5 million goes directly to primary prevention projects (PPPs) in various counties; the other $600,000 pays for administrative costs as well as the provision of two training centers to consult with PPPs delivering school-based prevention programs.

The legislation declares that

> child abuse and neglect is a severe and increasing problem in California. School districts and preschools are able to provide an environment for training of children, parents, and all school district staff. Primary prevention programs in the school districts are an effective and cost-efficient method of reducing the incidence of child abuse and neglect and for promoting healthy family environments. To ensure comprehensive and effective primary prevention education to all of California's public school children, it is the intent of the Legislature to provide adequate funding for training for each child four times in their school career, including once in preschool, elementary school, junior high school, and senior high school. It is the intention of the Legislation that primary prevention training for all children in publicly funded preschool through 12th grades, be encouraged in the school district system and preschools by the funding of appropriate agencies to provide the training.

The CAPTA program has no sunset clause, and therefore enjoys relatively protected funding for some years to come.

Child Abuse Prevention Nomenclature

The fledgling child abuse prevention field lacks a nomenclature to discuss programs delivered at schools. They are, at times, referred to generically as *CAP* (child assault prevention) programs even though CAP is a specific type of curriculum. In California, they are called CAPTA programs after the legislation that funds them. Neither name truly describes the locus or delivery of the program. We propose the following terms for clarity. *Classroom child abuse prevention* programs are those that are delivered to one classroom of students at a time. These programs are typically *visitor-delivered* programs insofar as they are provided by staff from outside agencies. Alternately, some are *teacher-delivered*: that is, provided by a school employee who typically teaches health or family life education. *School-level* programs are those that take the school as the locus of child abuse prevention and work to alter the characteristics of the school, its staff, and its students in a way that better protects adolescents. A school-level approach may, naturally, include classroom presentations that are either visitor- or teacher-delivered. *Community-based* approaches are those that also strive to strengthen protective factors in the community. A community-based approach may include school involvement by, for example, working to keep the school open on Friday and Saturday nights so youth have a place to go that is safe. This chapter's review of research on child abuse prevention considers only classroom-based programs and primarily covers visitor-delivered programs, the current norm. (Later, we consider school-level and community-based approaches.)

CAPTA

CAPTA's funding structure facilitates the support of independent community-based agencies to become PPPs (although school districts can also apply to be PPPs and deliver prevention classes in schools). It gives priority to community-based organizations to receive CAPTA funds, but does not require that they send in visitors to deliver the prevention services themselves or that they use a classroom-centered approach. These have been, however, far and away the most common choices. CAPTA funding initially supported a collection of eighty-four PPPs that were for the most part brand new. Except for a few influential programs that had been funded earlier through Office of Criminal Justice Planning or private sources, the majority of these programs had to establish new plans for delivering a new curricula quickly in order to gain support. In addition, fewer than 25 percent of the PPPs had experience providing prevention programs to children prior to when they began their high school level programs. Only a few programs in the state had any experience specifically providing prevention programs to high school students prior to 1986. Therefore, according to staff at OCAP, in most PPPs adolescent child abuse prevention programming began in 1985 or 1986 (Aurora Dominguez, personal communication, September 1987).

All programs chose to rely on classroom presentations. The PPPs use a diverse collection of approaches in their curricula. The majority of programs were described by OCAP as belonging to one of three equivalent-sized groupings: (1) those ascribing to the Child Assault Program (CAP) model (which was developed out of a feminist women's rape prevention program); (2) those "independent" of any formal curriculum; and (3) those "derivative" programs having a combination of CAP and other philosophies. Among the last, less than 10 percent affiliated with the Seattle model (Beland and Bak 1986), roughly 6 percent tried to combine the CAP model and the Seattle model with their own independent ideas, and about 5 percent used the Children's Self-Help model (1983) out of San Francisco. Remaining derivative programs were described as containing various other combinations of the models mentioned above.

In most cases, the curriculum *philosophies* that were developed for elementary age students were adopted whole cloth for high school students (Aurora Dominguez, personal communication, September 1987). Indeed, high school–level prevention programs in the vast majority of PPPs was the last to be developed, coming after the establishment of preschool, elementary, and middle school programs. PPPs typically borrowed concepts from programming used with younger children for their new high school curricula. The same emphases that were seen with elementary and preschool age children, such as "say no" and "go tell," were put into place with few alterations in high schools (Vivian Chavez and Hershel Swinger, personal communications, September 1987). Our interviews with providers in other states suggest that this is an often-used strategy for developing programs for adolescents.

Perhaps the most fundamental assumption of all child abuse prevention programs is that children are victims and not perpetrators of abuse. Indeed, arguments that children have any responsibility in abuse whatsoever have been soundly rejected by most program developers. Yet, as chapter 1 described, any sizable population of adolescents will include victims and perpetrators. The design of adolescent programs has generally not incorporated this key difference between adolescents and younger children. Because of this and other special characteristics of adolescents, results of abuse prevention programs for children can suggest what will result from programs delivered to adolescents, but they cannot provide great assurance.

Child Abuse Prevention Research

California's universal and repeated visitor-delivered classroom presentations to prevent adolescent abuse arose because of grave concern about child abuse, not because of any evidence that it would work. The basic assumptions of the approach is that children at all ages and in all families risk child abuse and that the more often the content was discussed, the greater the likelihood of preventing abuse. To date, research directed at school-based prevention programs has not been with high school students, but has instead assessed preschool and elementary grade children (Finkelhor 1986). Even these evaluations of prevention efforts with younger children are at the beginning stages of inquiry; findings are often contradictory (Finkelhor 1986). There were simply no published evaluations of high school child abuse prevention programs at the time this program began in California, and there were still none to be found as of the end of 1989.

Most studies of child abuse prevention with younger children have demonstrated only minor or moderate gains in knowledge. Small knowledge gains of no more than 2 percent were reported by Binder and McNeil (1987) and by Harvey, Forehand, Brown, and Holmes (1988), for example. Moderate knowledge gains were found by Wurtele, Saslawsky, Miller, Marrs, and Britcher (1986), Kraizer and Fryer (1988), and Fryer, Kraizer, and Miyoshi (1987a). Conte, Rosen, Saperstein, and Shermack (1985), on the other hand, identified gains of about 45 percent in their study of a prevention program with older children. Studies of preschool populations have found only marginal gains in knowledge (e.g., Borkin and Frank 1986; Gilbert et al. 1989; Liddell, Young, and Yamagishi 1988). Even more modest gains in knowledge have not always reflected measurable gains in behavior (Stilwell, Lutzker, and Greene 1988).

Older children have been reported to have relatively larger gains than their younger counterparts. In several studies, older elementary age children were found to score higher in knowledge following instruction than their younger counterparts (Conte et al. 1985; Sigurdson, Doig, and Strang 1985); Wurtele et al. 1986). This is consistent with developmental theory (Berrick and Gilbert in press). Yet, some researchers have found small initial gains in knowledge even among older children (Fryer, Kraiser, and Myoshi 1987a).

The bulk of research on prevention programs measures only the retention of knowledge; few attempts have been made to measure behavioral change (Levanthal 1987). Poche, Bouwer and Swearingen (1981) and Fryer, Kraizer, and Miyoshi (1987a, 1987b) indicated that preschool and early elementary school students showed enhanced resistance to abduction efforts by strangers. Indeed, child abuse prevention programs rarely teach resistance skills at all (Finkelhor 1986). If a child does not know how to handle situations to avoid or stop abuse, that youth may not take any of the appropriate actions she or he needs to take to implement the knowledge about abuse. Blending the teaching of intended skills, attitudes, and knowledge together effectively is a current challenge to child abuse prevention educators. The authors' study queries students about the actions they would intend to take in abuse-related situations and whether they used the skills after training.

In all, the vast majority of evaluations have no follow-up, and those that have followed and retested students generally show disappointing results. Borkin and Frank's (1986) evaluation of a program delivered to three-, four-, and five-year-old children found that less than 50 percent of the children retained any of the information provided in the program. Plummer (1984) found that fifth graders lost a significant amount of their initial learn-

ings by eight months after the prevention material was presented
to them. These results underscore the need for the kind of
follow-up that this study contains. Ray (1984) found that third
graders seemed especially to forget knowledge that contradicts
widespread social myths. As time went by students increasingly
began to believe that boys are not molested and that children are
usually molested by strangers. Both of these conceptions are
false: although parents tend to teach their children that strangers
are the ones who will molest them, 85 to 90 percent of victims
are molested by perpetrators familiar to them (Finkelhor 1986).
In a study of a sexual abuse prevention program with four- to
ten-year-old children, Conte et. al. (1985) found that the children over six retained more information than those under six.
Even the older children retained only about half of what they
were taught. Kolko, Moser, and Hughes (1989) found significant
gains in an awareness and skills-based sexual abuse prevention
program at posttraining and six-month follow-up.

In addition, few studies have looked for possible negative
effects of child abuse prevention programs. Recent findings on
younger children give some credence to the caution, at times
assumed to be reactionary, that prevention programs may cause
harm to children (Gilbert et al. 1988; Kraizer, 1986; Levanthal
1987). Swan, Press, and Briggs (1985) found that 7 percent of
the children in one program did not like the presentation, and
that 5 percent had adverse reactions. Garbarino (1986) found
that girls reported having more fearful reactions to a program
than boys. Miller-Perrin and Wurtele (1986) report that 11 percent of parents reported negative changes in their K–6-grade
children's behavior following a child abuse prevention videotape.
Our study probes for negative reactions amongst adolescents.

Shortcomings related to cultural and racial factors in the
child abuse prevention literature have been described. For example, Garbarino and Gilliam (1980) suggested that racial and socioeconomic factors cannot be considered separately in
prevention programs because class and ethnicity are often linked.
Korbin (1980) noted that variability within a culture can often
exceed crosscultural differences, emphasizing the importance of
closely examining the specific characteristics of cultures in the

study groups used in child abuse prevention research. Our study assesses the possibility of differential knowledge and learning for minority youth.

Another relatively underdeveloped area of child abuse prevention research consists of comparisons of instructional factors and strategies. Very little is known about the effect of such instructor variables as age, sex, ethnicity, education, and prior experience. Relatively little is known about the relative effect of such methodologies as discussion, role-play, lecture, film, and small group exercise. Slight attention has been given to the relationship of student population variables and these instruction variables (e.g., should classes have both male and female teachers?). The relationship between program length and effectiveness has not been well examined. A better relationship between research and program design may well be required before such variables can be examined. Close cooperation and trust is necessary to develop adequate research methodologies, with equivalent program and control comparison groups. Ideally, model programs could be set up that incorporate equivalent study groups that will facilitate later research from the beginning of program inception. Such efforts have not been reported in the literature. Our study does not remedy all lacunae in experimental design, but it does enlist a large and equivalent control group.

In California as well as in other states, high school students may receive some education regarding adolescent maltreatment in health and family life (sexuality) education classes. Some educators promote the incorporation of adolescent abuse prevention in family life education classes (Larrabee and Wilson 1981; Marion 1982). Curriculum and training on acquaintance rape and sexual abuse prevention are available and in use in some California health or family life education programs. A growing body of research indicates that family life education in high schools can effectively promote more appropriate parental values, generate more positive attitudes toward other people, influence intrafamily communication, improve self-esteem, and teach information about human sexuality (Cooke and Wallace 1984). Less clear is the effectiveness of such programs in ultimately changing behaviors. There is no evidence that family life programs are effective in preventing adolescent maltreatment or in preventing adolescents from becoming abusive themselves. Our review identified only one unpublished report that evaluated the teaching of pre-parenting education to a typical group of high school students in California, and assessed the effects on the likelihood of child abuse (Valentine-Dunham and Gipson 1980). Students were taught anger control techniques, stress management, and behavior management strategies. Students who received the training responded more favorably on paper to critical incidents involving toddlers that might provoke child abuse. Students' behavior in role-play situations was unchanged, however, and no assessments of the actual caregiving of a child were made.

All in all, high school child abuse prevention efforts now receive little guidance from descriptive or evaluative data. Still, family life programs have been introduced widely in mainstream classrooms as well as with special populations (Herz and Reis 1987; Schultz and Adams 1987) and the vast majority of students, parents, educators, and the general public favor offering family life education in the high schools (Arcus 1986). This evaluation will, then, consider the degree to which child abuse prevention content described and funded by the CAPTA legislation is integrated with family life classes.

Evaluations of programs that attempt to prevent child sexual abuse reveal that these programs often are built on untested assumptions (Reppucci and Haugaard 1989). Many prevention programs assume we know what prevention skills are most important, that knowledge alone transfers into effective action, and that the potential benefits outweigh the risks. The available evidence from child abuse prevention research is therefore largely drawn from samples of preschool and elementary age students and from studies with weak methodology. The current level of understanding is insufficient to discern if all or even if some of current school-based child maltreatment prevention programs really do help reduce child maltreatment. Serious concern still exists about long-term retention in all levels of prevention programs. We know little about which teachers and teaching methods are most effective with various student populations. Nor do we know if real changes in skills, behaviors, and knowledge occur. The potential impact and risks of school-based child abuse prevention programs for older children, including those attending high schools, is also uncertain. The relationship between program outcomes and the age and ethnicity level of the student; students' previous prevention-related classwork; and various influences of the family, community, and culture remains cloudy.

Preventing Adolescent Perpetration

Programs to combat adolescent acquaintance rape and acquaintance abuse are emerging. Most of the literature on acquaintance abuse is concerned with sexual abuse or rape and the bulk of the acquaintance rape literature relates to college age men and women. For want of research specific to adolescents, this literature is best able to inform this discussion.

Model programs are being developed to assist high school students who are also often exposed to sexual, physical, and psychological abuse in their relationships (Network against Teenage Violence 1987). Nelson and Clark (1986) describe the teen acquaintance rape project called *Alternatives to Fear*, designed in Seattle. In this program, girls are taught the difference between acceptable dating activities and date rape. Girls are also taught self-protection skills, given assertiveness training, and trained to use emotional intimacy as a guide for physical intimacy. Hughes and Sandler (1987) suggest that programs teach adolescent girls to understand their feelings about power, money, and sex; to be assertive; to use escape skills if necessary; to avoid drugs and undesirable locations; and to recognize danger signals. Evaluations are missing.

To our knowledge, only Charlene Muehlenhard and her colleagues has reported any successful outcome data with college students (Carlson, Muehlenhard and Julsonnet 1988; Flarity-White, Piper, and Muehlenhard 1988). No such studies address high school students. Their work indicates that repeated practice handling simulated date rape situations is essential to building prevention skills among females. In contrast, other investigators have shown no significant changes in attitudes as a result of programs that were brief and awareness—not practice—oriented (i.e., Borden, Karr, and Caldwell-Colbert 1988; Gottesman 1977; White and Nichols 1981). Although men are both perpetrators as well as victims of acquaintance abuse, most prevention efforts with college students are aimed at women. The majority of high school programs also focused on teaching about victimization and barely address males regarding perpetration of abuse (Carlson, Muehlenhard, and Julsonnet 1988).

In general, studies of adolescent sex offenders imply that early identification and treatment are necessary to prevent adolescents from developing lifelong patterns as sex offenders (Barnard et al. 1989; Becker, Cunningham-Rathner, and Kaplan 1986). Yet, although many programs have been described that serve identified adolescent sex offenders, programs to prevent adolescents from becoming abusive with peers or with younger children have rarely been delivered and no published evaluations exist. Little appears in the literature regarding assisting young males with the pressures they may feel to be sexually active. Programs for males teach them about stereotypical sex-role behaviors, alternative responses to girls' assertive behaviors, the differences between persuasion and coercion, and the meaning and value of open communication and boundaries in relationships (Hall and Kassees 1989; Nelson and Clark 1986).

Perhaps the best known program to prevent adolescents from becoming perpetrators is the five-day SHARP program of the Uptown Mental Health Center in Minneapolis (Mitnick 1989). The program considers it important to promote the values of equality and respect that help youth avoid domination and exploitation. A fundamental assumption is that to prevent child sexual abuse you must increase empathy for victims. A typology of adolescent sex offenders is then presented. This section also involves videotape vignettes of perpetrators discussing what they did, the disclosure of their perpetration, and the outcomes for them. The law is discussed so that no youth who completes the program can honestly claim what has been claimed by many perpetrators: that they did not know that what they did was illegal. A discussion of healthy decision making wraps up the program. The program has been used in classrooms, group homes, residential care facilities, juvenile detention facilities, and training schools.

Other Prevention Research

Although prior research with adolescent abuse prevention programs is virtually nil, extensive evaluations of efforts with adolescents to prevent substance abuse, pregnancy, smoking, delinquency, and sexually transmitted diseases offer ideas about abuse prevention. Many of these programs are brief, classroom-based efforts designed specifically for adolescent populations.

Critical Elements of Prevention Programs

Life skills training (or problem prevention) programs are ubiquitous. Most include from one to fifteen days of classroom instruction (Botvin 1986). The most effective programs include much role-play practice using the skills that are taught (e.g., Schinke and Gilchrist 1985). A few include homework assignments requiring practice of skills outside the classroom (Barth 1989). Helping adolescents to personalize the content so they believe that they are personally at risk is also essential (Barth, Middleton, and Wagman 1989). A few include booster sessions that remind students of what they learned within a reasonable time after the program. Programs that focus on changing the culture of the group may be most powerful (Fisher 1988; Moskowitz, in press). Longer interventions appear to have a greater chance of giving students the practice they need and in changing group culture, but just being a longer program is not a sufficient condition for success.

We also know something about program elements that do not appear to be helpful. Programs that focus on knowledge only find that increased knowledge is insufficient to increase student's ability to avoid problem behaviors (Kirby 1984; Williams, Ward, and Gray 1985). The usefulness of decision making and social problem-solving skills—as taught in the classroom—is also dubious (Tisdelle and St. Lawrence 1986). Experience *practicing* prosocial skills appears to enhance productive ways to think about problems more than teaching problem-solving *concepts* enhances productive ways of acting.

Type of Instruction

Theoretical and empirical reasons call for designers of prevention programs to consider peer influences on adolescents. Reviews of evaluations adolescent drug prevention programs indicated that peer-taught programs generally had more successful outcomes than adult-taught programs (Resnick 1983; Tobler, 1986). Peer influence is indeed one of the most important factors in the onset and maintenance of smoking, alcohol use, marijuana use, and tobacco chewing (Severson 1984). The significance of peers in assault situations has been shown earlier.

Although peer relationships are critical to adolescents, the success of peer-taught *child abuse* programs partly depends on the form of the program. Peer-teachers can be either "trained" by adults to act as social reinforcers and initiators, or simply introduced, "untrained," into the target population. Research shows that changing the behavior and responsiveness of peer leaders can result in changes in other peers. "Untrained" peer interventions appear unsuccessful, however, unless accompanied by social skills trainings provided by adults (Sancilio 1987). Botvin (1986) found that most of the successful substance abuse prevention programs that use social influence approaches also employ peer leaders. Perry et al. (1983) reported that successful smoking prevention programs also usually incorporate peer leaders either of the same age or older. The literature suggests that peer-teaching by trained peers can be particularly effective in training social skills, improving self-efficacy, and remediating deficiencies in skills (Shunk 1987). Yet, Shunk (1987) argues that the perceived similarity between model and observer is not as important as the perceived value of the behaviors being taught. Children tend to accept as models those they feel are competent and possess self-efficacy and behavioral appropriateness. Closeness in age is not a major factor: children do not appear to have a stronger inclination to model adults over peers. The sex of the peer model seems to influence the performance of children more than their learning, which suggests that teachers use both sexes in programs when possible. The similarity of the peer-model's background (home town, interests, school) to the target peers was found to foster learning, although there is insufficient evidence to determine exactly why.

Classes that are led by visiting experts, teachers, or peers have been compared in a few studies. For example, Clarke, MacPherson, Holmes, and Jones (1986) found that teacher-led approaches were somewhat more successful than peer-led approaches, particularly with females. Expert-led approaches were unsuccessful. They recommend developmentally based, teacher-led programs that include continuous reinforcement of learning objectives. Sandoval, Davis, and Wilson (1987) discuss possible dangers of using peer counseling with adolescent suicide prevention programs because of the adolescent's willingness to keep confidences and relative lack of experience about how to handle suicidal ideation and behaviors. The extension of this concern to child abuse is apparent.

Summary of Life Skills Training

In general, the technology for use in prevention skills training is now in its third era. In the first, knowledge of the existence and negative consequences of a condition like unprotected sex, drug use, or acquaintance rape was considered adequate to promote adolescents' well-being. These conventional prevention programs have had unimpressive outcomes (Forman and Neal 1987; Kirby 1984), yet the dominance of this approach endures. A recent review of adolescent pregnancy prevention programs (Stout and Rivara 1989) found little impact on what students do about birth control and sexuality after classroom presentations. As Stout describes: "There's nothing unique about transmitting information about sex as opposed to algebra or History 101; kids don't take one math course and become engineers and rocket scientists ("Education doesn't change behavior" 1989, p. A1).

The second era included attention to affective, cognitive, and social skills training to increase the likelihood that students will use their knowledge. This is a promising, but still incomplete, approach, as we are not sure what skills to teach, how well they are learned, and how useful they will be (Barth, in press; Botvin 1986; Moskowitz, in press).

Recently, a few programs have entered a third era, characterized by attention to the school and community context of problems in living. For example, Solomon and DeJong (1986) report on impressive efforts to combat the spread of AIDS by attempting to influence the knowledge, attitudes, and behaviors of the target population through social marketing techniques, public health clinics, and other community awareness programs. Efforts to address external contributors to victimization of youth include such features as: comprehensive K–12 curriculum; developing caring climates and opportunities for responsibility and cooperation in schools; and linkages to the home and community (Bernard 1989; Zambrana and Aguirre-Molina 1987). The theory and practice of this approach outpaces its evaluation, which has just begun.

Conclusions

What can be learned from this prevention literature and applied to child abuse program research? First, the abuse of adolescents is in many ways less emphasized as a social problem than the abuse of other ages. The bulk of the literature regarding child abuse is concerned with younger children, particularly elementary age children. The greatest effort to prevent acquaintance abuse is with college age students.

Second, prevention priorities may not reflect current knowledge of victim characteristics and prevention strategies. Efforts to prevent the abuse of adolescents appear to emphasize the protection of potential victims rather than the prevention of adolescents from becoming abusive themselves. In addition, efforts overwhelmingly emphasize the protection of females, although many males are victims of maltreatment and are probably even less likely to report their maltreatment than females. Males also perpetrate assaults at a rate far higher than females. Although little is known about the relative impact of various forms of abuse on adolescents, most prevention efforts emphasize prevention of sexual abuse over physical abuse, neglect, and psychological maltreatment. Many programs borrowed strategies employed with younger children (say no and go tell) or older populations (women's rape movement curricula) instead of developing curricula and teaching strategies that reflect the unique developmental needs and interests of adolescents.

Third, ultimately the true test of success in any prevention program must be in the area of behavior change. The teaching of knowledge or the changing of attitudes does not necessarily bring about desired behavioral changes in prevention programs. What does change behavior seems to be making students aware of negative social influences, correcting misconceptions that reinforce negative behaviors and ensuring practice in using the skills in classroom and community-based exercises. No one counsels against providing information or working with attitudes, but most everyone agrees that multiple teaching goals are most desirable.

Fourth, many methods of school-based prevention with adolescents have been used, but paltry evaluation efforts leave their relative strengths and weaknesses obscured. Most researchers and theorists seem to suggest that multilevel approaches be incorporated in prevention programs in terms of teaching techniques, teaching goals, and teachers. Teaching techniques should involve students actively in the classroom and should include role-play, lecture, discussion, modeling, and rehearsal, as well as perhaps computer instruction and other creative methods. Teaching goals should incorporate outcomes in all ecological areas, including the affective, cognitive, psychomotor (e.g., escape skills) and socioenvironmental (i.e., modifying the home, school, or other living environments).

Concern has been expressed by many professionals that teachers of prevention programs better reflect the ethnic, cultural, and gender diversity of the students they serve. There is a lack of consensus on whether the most competent teachers are peers, outside experts, or high school staff. The influence of peers on adolescents and the success of peer-taught substance abuse programs is, however, relatively well documented. Some experts recommend using a combination of peers, experts, and high school staff. Evidence suggests that adolescent prevention curricula should, at least in some cases, be initiated with children as young as those in the sixth grade, and then reinforced and elaborated on throughout the adolescent years. The degree of reinforcement (which is related to program length and extent of follow-up) appears related to success. In addition, experts would agree that no single approach to prevention works for all situations; strategies should be designed with the local target population and environment in mind (Goodstadt 1987). The emerging consensus is that prevention strategies for one adolescent problem area need to be related to prevention efforts for other problem areas—just as the problems of substance misuse and violence are related.

Finally, little consensus guides determination of the level of measured increases in knowledge, skills, or attitudes required to claim success in adolescent prevention programs. For example, in smoking prevention evaluations, reductions of 33 to 39 percent in the proportion of individuals beginning to smoke, of 43 to 47 percent of prevalence of regular smoking, and of 29 to 67 percent of prevalence of experimental smoking have been reported as indicating success (Botvin 1986). In child abuse prevention programs for younger children, success has been claimed when 31 percent of eighty-three children answered one question "What would you do if someone tries to touch you in a way that doesn't feel good?" correctly (Borkin and Frank 1986). Studies range in the significance of knowledge gain from .1 percent increase (Binder and McNeil 1987) to a 20 percent gain (Wurtele, Marrs, and Miller-Perrin 1987) and even higher (Conte et al. 1985). Because no definitive relationship between knowledge gain and behavior change has been established, the debate about the meaningfulness of change will continue in this book.

3
Methods

O ur study describes the various approaches to child abuse prevention programs in high schools in California, and estimates their effectiveness in preventing adolescent abuse. A number of critical and previously unexamined areas were investigated. First, we examined the nature of high school prevention programs and the goals and methods of their curricula in the California CAPTA programs and, for comparison, in other states. The effectiveness of the high school CAPTA programs in teaching students new skills, knowledge, and behaviors to avoid abuse was assessed with student questionnaires and by interviews with students, parents, CAPTA staff, high school staff, and child protective service and law enforcement staff. The retention of this learning was tested. The impact of child abuse prevention programs on high school youth from various cultural and ethnic groups; on school personnel, parents, and protective service and law enforcement agencies; and on relationships between various school and community-level prevention efforts was estimated.

Theory and Conceptual Framework

A number of expected relationships were developed and tested. These expected relationships arise from learning theory, child development theory, ecological theory, and extent (albeit scant) prevention literature. Student characteristics and program characteristics may predict the outcomes of child abuse prevention training (see table 3–1). Student characteristics included sex, ethnicity, social and economic status (estimated by mother's level of

Table 3–1
Student and Program Characteristics and Outcomes

Student and Program Type	Outcomes
Student Characteristics	Student Learning
Sex	Types of maltreatment
Ethnicity	Intended skill areas
Mother's education (SES)	Attitude areas
Prior CAPTA-like classes	Knowledge areas
Program Characteristics	Program Impact
Group (program or control)	Student assessments
Methodology (peer or adult)	Parental assessments
Length of program	Professional assessments

education), and prior child abuse prevention education. There were three types of program characteristics, each of which described a dimension of the study group (program or control), teaching method (only in the case of the San Francisco PPP which compared either peer-taught and adult-taught), and length of program (in hours).

The study includes two broad areas of outcome: (1) the learning of program content and (2) program impact, as assessed by the students, their parents, and selected professionals in the categories described above. The learning of program content by students include measures of initial gains in attitudes, knowledge, and intended skills in the content areas identified in the CAPTA legislation. Student, parental, and professional assessments included measures of reported change in student learning and willingness to report child abuse, changes in levels of student anxiety, coordination of services between organizations, appropriateness of reporting student disclosures of abuse, and changes in student assertiveness. The study hypotheses developed these concepts:

1. Overall, some initial gain in student knowledge, attitudes, and intended skills can be expected. Findings from evaluations of other high school level prevention programs—smoking (Evans 1988; Killan 1985), pregnancy (Proctor 1986; Starn and Paperny 1986), and

substance abuse (Botvin 1986; Horan and Williams 1982; Schinke and Gilchrist 1985; Severson 1984), for example—show at least some initial gains. Similarly, modest gains were also found in evaluations of elementary level child abuse prevention programs (for example, Fryer, Kraizer, and Miyoshi 1987a; Plummer 1984; Ray 1984).

2. Changes in knowledge, attitudes, and intended skills will decline as time elapses from training. These results will depend on the interaction among three influences: (1) forgetting, (2) sensitization to other child abuse material that students are exposed to in extraprogram activities, and (3) maturation of the adolescents in the evaluation.

3. Initial learning gain and retention will differ among the various subscales. These differences may reflect societal tendencies as well as program emphases. Concepts reinforced by school and society will tend to have higher initial gains and better retention. Similarily, content that represents preconceptions of students (that reflect common societal myths about child abuse) may tend to remain unchanged, because people tend to believe what they are first taught. Curriculum areas that conflict with preconceptions of youth because of different culture, ethnicity, or gender experience may show reduced initial gains and long-term retention.

4. Program emphases and teaching strategies will influence scores. Devotion of greater time and repetition to a curriculum area foretells greater gains and retention. We expected that students in high school CAPTA programs with longer class time will learn more, because they have greater exposure to and reinforcement of the material. As discussed earlier and supported by learning theory, practice is also critical to learning and remembering (Bandura 1977). Programs that involve students in practice role-plays—more than those that demonstrate role-plays, or only discuss content—will more effectively teach self-protection skills. Teaching techniques that use powerful models for adolescents, such as the use of peer teachers,

are compatible with adolescent development and likely to result in greater learning.

5. Initial gains, retention, and satisfaction of students will vary with student characteristics. Students with prior exposure to child abuse prevention content will tend to learn more than those without exposure, because the repetition of much of the material will reinforce learning. Females will also tend to score higher, because they are viewed as the most likely victims of adolescent abuse and consequently receive more warnings about victimization. Minority students will tend to score lower when programs overlook cultural differences or don't have minority teachers. Children from less-educated families will (when other things are held constant) tend to score lower, because they may have received less home instruction.

Project Design and Method

The effectiveness of CAPTA high school programs was evaluated in terms of students' self-reported attitudes related to child abuse, knowledge about the definitions of various forms of child abuse and how to protect themselves, and intended prevention skills. The observations of students, parents, and various professionals regarding learned attitudes, knowledge, and intended skills of students and the impact of the programs on the family, school, and child protective service system were also recorded. Qualitative and quantitative techniques for data collection were used. Initially a content analysis of materials was carried out to develop a typology of program approaches. This analysis, however, contributed little basis for selection of study sites because no useful typologies were identified on the basis of curricula alone. As will be seen, the curricula from the various PPPs included many topic areas, with as many differences as similarities among programs in the states.

As an alternative to selecting types of programs, the study sought representative programs. A number of research strategies were used to identify important program characteristics for inclusion in the sample. These included meeting with providers, reviewing informal or published curricula, and surveying PPPs in the state. Six sets of factors that distinguish high school child abuse prevention programs were identified: content area, teaching methodology, program length, program locale, orientation, and purpose.

About a dozen possible study sites were initially identified along with other demographic considerations (including a balance of programs in northern and southern California and a balance of rural, urban, and suburban programs). Because most high school level programs were relatively new (less than three years old, and in many cases still in formation) an effort was made to choose the oldest, most stable programs. Whereas professionals from across the state believed that overall differences in philosophy about prevention existed between northern and southern California, a strong effort was made to select sites from both regions. Although the bulk of population in California is in urban areas, a significant portion exists in rural and agricultural regions. Therefore, one site was in a rural county and one in a largely agricultural county. (The inclusion of these sites also improves the generalizability of our results to the nation.) In recognition of California's three largest urban areas, potential program sites were initially approached in each of the San Diego, Los Angeles, and San Francisco areas. Unfortunately, the prevention programs we contacted in San Diego County were unable to obtain permission from key local school systems to participate in the project.

Study Sites

Final sites were selected so that the sample would be as representative of California's diverse population as possible and reflect the strongest programs. Programs were sought that targeted tenth graders, because tenth grade is the modal grade level for teaching high school level prevention programs and family life education. A broad selection of innovative program curricula and methodologies was also sought. Finally, programs that were mature and well regarded by their peers and by State Office of Child Abuse personnel were given preference. The six final programs selected included (1) a peer-teaching approach, (2) a skill-based curriculum, (3) a nationally recognized program that emphasizes student self-defense, (4) a program that uses a curriculum originally based on feminist, rape prevention strategies, (5) a program particularly interactive with the school system, and (6) an eclectic curriculum.

Although some of the original dozen sites selected were not able to be a part of the study (primarily because the schools were unwilling to accept the additional burden of participation), six study sites eventually agreed to participate. They were: Touch Safety Program, San Rafael, Marin County; Children's Self-Help, San Francisco; Think Smart Be Safe, Intercommunity Guidance Center, Whittier, Los Angeles County; Primary Prevention Program, Woman's Center of San Joaquin County, Stockton; Placer Woman's Center, Auburn, Placer County; and the Rape Treatment Center, Santa Monica, Los Angeles County. Each of the programs attempted to have a parent's program, although none of the programs claimed more than a 5 percent turnout rate of parents.

The Touch Safety Program in the Marin program emphasized acquaintance rape, assertiveness training, and definition and dynamics of child abuse, and provided a two-day program, fifty minutes each day. Project staff taught the programs, using discussion, role-plays, and media.

San Francisco's Children's Self-Help Project had both a peer-taught and adult-taught program running concurrently at the same high school. This enabled a comparison to be made between the effectiveness of both groups. The peer-taught group contained thirty-four students, the adult-taught group contained twenty students, and the control group had sixty students. Observations confirmed that both program groups used essentially the same curriculum, so that the primary difference between the groups was the age of the presenters. The two-day (fifty minutes a day) San Francisco program emphasized children's rights, dealing with peer pressure, sexual abuse, and trust your feelings. The program relied on discussion and presentation.

The Primary Prevention Program of Stockton program emphasized acquaintance rape, assertiveness, and personal rights.

The program was delivered in one, fifty-minute class. Discussion, media, and presentation were enlisted.

In Auburn, the national award winning Placer Women's Center program gave students a three-day program, with fifty minutes each day. Self-defense, acquaintance rape, and sexual abuse were emphasized, although many topics were covered. The Auburn staff invited a police officer to teach self-defense, had the mother of a sexual abuse victim speak, and used presentation and discussion.

In Los Angeles, the Whittier Intercommunity Guidance Center program emphasized the definition and dynamics of child abuse (the first priority), empowerment, and trust your feeling. The three-day, fifty minute-each-day program utilized media, discussion, and presentation.

The Santa–Monica based Rape Treatment Center program was a three-day program with one hour of teaching provided each day. Acquaintance rape, sexual abuse, and children's rights were emphasized in the program, which utilized media, discussion, and presentation.

Research Design and Procedures

This study was conducted over a two-year period and had three primary components: (1) a self-report component with three observations—pretest, posttest (immediately after the program), and follow-up (three to five months after the program); (2) interviews of students, parents, and professionals; and (3) a survey of key informants. Each observation point included a program group and a control group of students at each high school. The program group was given the CAPTA program before the posttest, while the control group did not receive their program until after the posttest. Each control group received the program shortly after the posttest and well before the follow-up, using a crossover design. The crossover was essential to the overall design because of the need to compare control and program groups and to provide all youth with child abuse prevention content. Practical considerations did not allow a program to give CAPTA classwork to only some students in a school setting. The use of this design allowed for comparison of outcomes for students who did and did not receive the training. Follow-up testing was also completed but, given this design, does not permit comparisons at follow-up between the experiences of trained and untrained students—by that time, all students had been trained. Follow-up does tell how much students recalled and used their instruction. Overall, comparisons can be made between: (1) scores of both groups in the gains from pretest to posttest; (2) posttest to follow-up gain scores for students in the program group; and (3) pretest to follow-up gain scores for all students. In the second component of the study, a series of interviews provided additional data from selected high school students, teachers, parents, and helping professionals.

The evaluation also included a range of efforts to learn from key informants. All child abuse prevention programs in the state were sent surveys that were designed to help describe the nature of adolescent prevention programs. Professionals from other states were interviewed to determine the nature of adolescent prevention programs in those states. Family life and health educators in a number of states, including California, were interviewed to determine the extent and manner of inclusion of adolescent abuse prevention in other high school classes. After study sites were selected, the high school administrators and teachers were contacted and discussions were held regarding methods of assessment. Passive consent forms were designed for the self-report assessments and delivered to high school teachers. Consent was also received in writing from high school administrators at each school site. Procedures were arranged beforehand with high school staff regarding the assessments. An introductory statement was prepared to be read by whomever administered the questionnaires, which described the purpose and confidentiality of the evaluation and asked students to answer the questions as honestly as possible. An inquiry was made to the California Attorney General's office to clarify reporting responsibilities. Project staff were also trained by the author regarding assessment and child abuse reporting procedures.

At each of the study sites, arrangements were made with

Table 3–2
Design for Collection of Self-Report Data

Program	Pretest	CAPTA	Posttest		Follow-up
Group	(n = 251)		(n = 247)		(n = 133)
Control	Pretest		Posttest	CAPTA	Follow-up
Group	(n = 200)		(n = 196)	(crossover)	(n = 111)
Elapsed	1st day	2–3 days	1 week	2 weeks	4–5 months
Time					

providers of the curriculum and with school personnel to assign at least one class to be a program group and at least one class to be a control group. Passive consent forms were sent home from school. Only two phone calls were received from parents who had additional questions or concerns.

Classes chosen at each school were as equivalent as possible; for example, in one school two family life classes were selected, with similar student composition. In another school, both groups were drawn from similar physical education classes. As can be seen in table 3–2, 443 students took the pretest and first post-test. Of these, 244 students (about 55 percent of the total) took the follow-up. This decrease was due to student transfers, scheduling difficulties, and lack of continued interest of some of the students in the study. The breakdown of the sample by site is shown in table 3–3.

Table 3–3
*Sample Size of Self-Report Assessment for Pretest and Posttest**

PPPs	*Program Groups*	*Control Groups*	*Total n*	*Percent of Total*
San Francisco	54	60	114	26
Marin	24	18	42	9
Auburn	49	18	67	15
Stockton	27	8	35	8
LA Whittier	62	36	98	22
LA Santa Monica	31	56	87	20
TOTALS	247	196	443	100

*Includes students who completed pretests and posttests

Table 3–4
Sample Size of Self-Report Assessment for Students completing Follow-up

PPPs	Program Groups	Control Groups	Total n	Percent of Total
San Francisco	33	35	68	28
Marin	17	13	30	12
Auburn	31	14	45	18
Stockton	10	2	12	5
Whittier	23	12	35	7
Santa Monica	19	35	54	22
TOTALS	133	111	244	101*

*Column total does not equal 100 percent because of rounding error.

At each site, both classes of high school students were given paper and pencil pretest questionnaires by their own teacher or by a project staff member. They were first asked to describe various demographic characteristics of themselves and their families. Students were queried about their knowledge, attitudes, and skills related to prevention of adolescent abuse. All students in the program groups were given the class evaluation survey and the posttest questionnaire soon after receiving the program. At the same time, students in the control groups received only the posttest questionnaire. Finally, four to five months after the posttest, students in both groups were given the follow-up instrument. By follow-up, the sample size was reduced to 244 (see table 3–4). The pretest, posttest, and follow-up are identical, each with thirty-four-item questionnaires. All of these instruments are described in chapter 4.

Instrument Development

The centerpiece of the evaluation was the self-report assessment, completed by students from the six study sites. The self-report assessments consisted of questionnaires constructed by the study staff and distributed and collected by the researcher or by participating high school teachers. These questionnaires were designed to cover concepts common to prevention programs at all developmental levels and those specific only to high school programs, and were pilot-tested prior to the beginning of pretesting. The instruments were designed with the help of other researchers and consultants, and pilot-tested with help from the Children's Self-Help Project in San Francisco and the Stockton study site.

Content Development

The content for these self-report instruments (as well as the interview instruments described below) was taken from the goals of the CAPTA legislation, originally implemented through AB 2443 in October 1984. The goals of CAPTA are clearly stated in the law, which has been amended a number of times since AB 2443. Two training centers were established to assist in the initial and ongoing training of the primary prevention projects, as well as to encourage voluntary participation by schools and communities. The primary prevention projects were given the mandate to provide workshops for students, parents, and teachers that are culturally, linguistically, and age appropriate. The workshops for teachers and parents were to cover indicators of abuse, crises counseling, and reporting. Workshops for students were to cover the right to live free of abuse, disclosure, support services, safety, and self defense. In addition, the students were to be given sessions after their programs that provided (as appropriate) crises counseling, disclosure, and reporting.

Consultations were also held with the staff of both regional child abuse prevention training centers, which are funded by the state to provide consultation to the local projects. During a meeting with the staff from the southern training center, for example, a dozen PPP administrators met with training center staff and project staff to discuss the design of the instrument. A number of northern training center staff were also interviewed regarding the instrument design.

In all, the development of the pretest, posttest, and follow-up forms of the self-report instrument and scoring procedures for all items was a team effort by a multidisciplinary group of child abuse, education, and child development experts. The high school project staff had extensive experience that contributed to the instrument development. Many professionals were consulted in developing the self-report instrument. Initially, local experts in education and psychotherapy were contacted, including an innovative and recognized prevention educator and a pioneering and leading family life educator.

Staff from all six PPP study sites also participated in designing the instruments. Some PPP administrators met with the project staff and went over the instrument item by item. Other administrators were mailed updated versions of the instrument for their feedback. In addition, additional PPP administrators who did not participate in the study were consulted.

Various nationally known experts in child abuse were also consulted. Copies of the third draft of the instrument were mailed to members of academia and the professional community for their inspection. Perspectives of minority populations were also considered in this process. A number of black, Hispanic, and Asian professionals, including some of those described above, provided the author with their comments to help ensure sensitivity to culture and race in the instrument.

Pilot-testing

The self-report instruments were pilot-tested with a culturally and ethnically mixed group of students in San Francisco. To minimize any bias related to reading ability, staff first tried to read the items out loud to students. It was soon determined, however, that this method was undesirable: many of the students reacted to the items as they were read, and appeared to influence other students in the room. The decision was made to let students read the items silently at their own pace, after the instructions were read to them. A multicultural group of students who read the questionnaires to themselves reported that they found the items generally easy to understand and enjoyable. The high school teacher who was in the room recommended that the regular teacher be in the room when questionnaires were given.

In conclusion, a multidisciplinary, multiracial team of professionals and lay people, from the local, state, and national levels, were consulted throughout the process of instrument design. Those consulted included high school teachers and counselors, parents, high school students, academic researchers, child abuse experts, child development experts, child abuse prevention and treatment educators, therapists, and PPP staff. This instrument, which is the first of its kind (except for some brief self-evaluations developed by programs) can be further improved. Still, by the standards of conventional social science, content validity and face validity of this instrument are reasonably guaranteed.

Content of Self-Report Measures

Demographics

In the student self-report instruments, the measures that were designed to operationalize the independent variables included demographic items, questionnaire items for the pretest and posttests, and class evaluation items. The demographic items (shown in full along with all student self-report measures in appendix A) included simple measures of gender, ethnicity, number of parents at home, previous abuse prevention class experience, sources of family income, and mother's education. Students were simply asked for their own estimation to each response. The authors recognize that some students would not have precise knowledge of family income and, so, used rather broad categories.

Pretest, Posttest, and Follow-up

The pretest, posttest, and follow-up used the same thirty-four items. These items are summarized in table 3–5.

Types of Items

Three types of measures were constructed in the pretest and posttests: vignettes with multiple choice responses, fill-in-the-blank items, and Likert scale items. In all cases, students were asked to respond as honestly as possible, and were reassured about individual confidentiality. The *multiple choice* vignettes,

Table 3–5
Student Self-Report Items

Number	Item	Type*	Measure**
1	Mother always yelling at teen.	MC	IS
2	Stepfather slaps teen boy while drunk.	MC	IS
3	Older brother tries to molest sister.	MC	IS
4	Teen boy wants sex with young girl.	MC	IS
5	Parents always fighting with each other.	MC	IS
6	Teen mother feels like hitting her child.	MC	IS
7	Man asks teen boy for sex.	MC	IS
8	Two places to call if you are abused.	FB	K
9	Two people to go to if you are abused.	FB	K
10	Girlfriend tells you she was molested.	FB	IS
11	Sister's boyfriend pressuring her for sex.	FB	IS
12	How can teen boy stop hitting his girl?	FB	IS
13	Baby-sitting teen suspects baby neglected.	FB	IS
14	Girl's parents emotionally abusing her.	L	A
15	Guy has to pressure girl for sex.	L	A
16	If boy is molested by man he will be gay.	L	K
17	Girls cannot tell boys thoughts on sex.	L	A
18	Boys cannot be sensitive and caring.	L	A
19	Guys should have final say.	L	A
20	Should you report a past incident?	L	K
21	Father physically hits boy with belt.	L	A
22	Aunt sexually touches her teen nephew.	L	A
23	Teen forced to miss school to baby-sit.	L	A
24	Teen boy hits girlfriend and apologizes.	L	A
25	Teen boy is turned on by young girl.	L	A
26	Teen boy in item 25 now touches girl.	L	A
27	Teen girl neglected; kicked out of house.	L	A
28	Where can girl in item 27 go for help?	FB	K
29	Teens are abused more by strangers.	L	K
30	Date rape happens to girl at party.	L	A
31	Did girl in item 30 lead boy on?	L	A

Table 3–5 (*continued*)

Number	Item	Type*	Measure**
32	Did girl in item 30 like the experience?	L	A
33	Critical father emotionally abusive.	L	A
34	Father physically abusive: beats up son.	L	A

**MC = multiple choice; FB = fill in the blank; L = Likert (1 = strongly agree, 2 = agree, 3 = disagree, 4 = strongly disagree)
**Measures: IS = intended skill; K = knowledge; A = attitude.

items 1 through 7, described abusive situations students were likely to encounter. Students were asked to choose one of four or five responses that describe alternative behaviors (response skills) an adolescent could make when faced with the situation described. These items attempted to measure behaviors that are taught in CAPTA programs. These items were recorded so that the most desirable answer, generally one judged to be the most assertive response, was given a value of 3. The next most desirable response was generally judged passive or neutral, and was given a score of 2. The least desirable response, where violence was likely to be further escalated through an aggressive behavior, was given a value of 1.

With the *fill-in-the-blank* items (8 to 13 and 28), students were asked to write in a response to each question, which involved either knowledge or intended skill. These items attempt to measure knowledge of community resources or alternative skills taught in the CAPTA programs. These items were scored either with a value of 2 (for a desirable response) or 1 (for an undesirable response). Many items had multiple desirable responses. With items that had two parts, numbers 8, 9, 11, and 12, the scores from both parts were added together to create a new variable.

The *Likert* scale items (14 through 27 and 29 through 34) had a format of statement or question followed by four ordered responses: strongly disagree, disagree, agree, and strongly agree. These items attempted to measure either attitudes or knowledge taught by programs. The most desirable response was coded 4, the next desirable 3, the next desirable 2, and the least desirable 1.

Measures of Intended Skill, Knowledge, and Attitude

In items that measured *intended skills,* students were given short vignettes that described typical abusive situations that many adolescents face. Students were asked to consider how the adolescent should act in each situation by selecting the most appropriate response from those provided. These items are conceptualized as *intended skills* because there is no assurance that the self-protection behaviors or skills tapped by the items actually reflect how the respondents would act in real-life situations.

In items that measured *knowledge,* students were provided with fill-in-the-blank or Likert scale items that required responses about facts that are essential to adolescent abuse prevention. Thus, students were asked to identify key community resources, information on the reporting law, or information about the results of rape of males. *Attitudinal* items essentially required students to consider what they thought about various key issues of adolescent abuse. Some of the items asked students to report on their attitudes regarding appropriate dating behaviors. Other items asked students to decide to what extent certain described situations constitute adolescent abuse.

Data Management

In general, the construction of measures of the independent variables in the self-report instruments was followed by systematic cleaning and recording of the data as well as the preparation of subscales. All items were coded or recorded so that desired responses were arranged in the same order. Items were not included in scale construction when they did not have sufficient scatter, and responses with low scores were combined with other scores as appropriate.

Consumer Satisfaction

The Class Evaluation instrument (see appendix A) gave students an opportunity to directly evaluate the CAPTA program they were given. The instrument used mostly Likert scale items to measure responses of students to various statements about the program (see table 3–6). In the Likert items, students had the choice of four responses: strongly disagree, disagree, agree, strongly agree. One fill-in-the-blank item (L) and two multiple choice items (M and N) were also included. All scale items were recorded when necessary so that the most positive response was coded 4, the next desirable coded 3, the next 2, and the least desirable coded 1.

Scale Construction

One goal of the study was to construct scales that represented the various curricular areas taught in the programs. The first

Table 3–6
Class Evaluation Survey Items

Number	Item	Item Type
A	I learned a lot from the class.	Likert
B	The class was boring.	Likert
C	We had time to ask questions and discuss.	Likert
D	We were told we could talk alone with an adult.	Likert
E	I felt comfortable with the things we discussed.	Likert
F	This information will help me.	Likert
G	I could understand the information.	Likert
H	The class will make teens worry too much.	Likert
I	I am now less likely to be abused.	Likert
J	I am now more likely to report abuse.	Likert
K	If I were abused, I would still not report it.	Likert
L	If you would still not report, why not?	Blanks
M	In what grade should this class first be given?	Multiple Choice
N	What was the best part of the class?	Multiple Choice
O	I wish I had had this information before.	Likert
P	I found the information helpful.	Likert
Q	The information helped me recognize a victim.	Likert

step in this process was the application of factor analysis to the data. Six factor clusters were identified, using Likert scale items from the pretest questionnaire, with Eigenvalues from 3.5 through 1.1 (see table 3–7).

Four scales were developed from these factors, and using the child abuse literature as a basis, four more scales were added. The major areas of adolescent abuse described in the literature include physical abuse, neglect, sexual abuse, psychological abuse, acquaintance rape, and self-identification of adolescents as potential abusers. In addition, other key areas identified in the literature were knowledge, intended skills, and attitudes.

All eight scales, and a ninth summary scale that included all items, were tested using reliability procedures (see table 3–8). Four scales had standardized item alphas higher than .60. All items together had an alpha of .80. The procedure found standardized item alpha levels of .70 for acquaintance rape, .64 for emotional abuse, and .61 for assertiveness. Three additional scales had lower alphas: .58 for physical abuse, .55 for community resources, and .37 for sexual abuse (which includes sexual abuse committed by adults). Two other attempts to construct scales clearly failed the reliability test: .26 for neglect and .18 for self-identification. Although these scales were retained for some purpose, their interpretation must be cautious.

The scales for acquaintance rape, emotional abuse, physical abuse, sexual abuse, and neglect essentially included items that related to each specific form of adolescent abuse. The assertive-

Table 3–7
Factor Analysis of Self-Report Items

Factor	Items in Factor	Percent of Variance	Eigen-value
Acquaintance Rape	15, 19, 30, 31, 32	17.4	3.5
Emotional Abuse	14, 19, 23, 24, 26, 33	9.2	1.8
Physical Abuse	21, 26, 27, 30, 33, 34	7.6	1.5
Sexual Abuse	16, 22, 25, 26	5.5	1.1

ness scale includes items that reflected knowledge, skills, and attitudes related to passive, assertive, and aggressive forms of response behaviors. The community resources scale measured the knowledge and attitudes students have related to whom they would go to for help. The acquaintance rape, emotional abuse, physical abuse, and sexual abuse scales had items that were included because of the factor analysis findings but they did not necessarily have face validity.

Three additional scales (table 3–8) were developed and tested for internal consistency. The skills scale included all items that measured the learning of skills taught in the CAPTA programs. The attitude scale included items that measured the attitudes learned. Finally, the knowledge scale included items that measured student learning of knowledge. A class evaluation scale with a standardized item alpha of .77 was developed from the class evaluation survey.

Table 3–8
Tests for Reliability

Scale	Final Items Included	Standardized Item Alpha
Acquaintance rape	15, 19, 30, 31, 32	.70
Emotional abuse	2, 14, 19, 23, 24, 26, 33	.64
Physical abuse	21, 26, 27, 30, 33, 34	.58
Sexual abuse	3, 7, 10, 22, 26	.37
Assertiveness	2, 3, 4, 5, 6, 7	.61
Community resources	8, 9, 10, 13, 28	.55
Neglect	13, 27, 28	.26
Self-Identification	4, 6, 12, 25, 26	.18
All	1–34	.80
Skill	1–7, 10–13	.61
Attitude	14, 15, 17–19, 21–27, 30–34	.70
Knowledge	8, 9, 16, 20, 28, 29	.52
Student evaluation	A–K, O–Q	.77

Interviews

Although a wealth of information was generated through the self-report assessments, the students were not given opportunity through the use of these instruments to explain in more detail what they thought about the child abuse prevention programs. In addition, the added perspective of their parents, as well as the various professionals in their communities responsible for their protection and education, had not been tapped. Therefore, interviews were included in the design to provide this additional and valuable information. Staff trainings were conducted by the project director in preparation for interviewing.

Students

Interviews ($n = 72$) were arranged with consent from the student and the parent. All student interviews were conducted by the authors or by project staff trained by the authors and used an instrument designed specifically for this purpose. Interviews were conducted at the school sites. From three to five months after the first posttest was completed (and after all students had received the programs) the schools were recontacted and interview schedules were set up. Interviewers visited the school and met with each youth individually for about twenty minutes. All students who agreed to be interviewed were interviewed. The sample of students, although about equally divided between boys and girls, also tended to include students who appeared unusually interested and well informed about adolescent prevention.

Parents

Parent interviews ($n = 23$) were conducted by phone in the weeks following the completion of student interviews. Consent for these interviews was incorporated into the consent form used for the student interviews. These interviews were also conducted by the authors or by staff trained by the authors, using an instrument designed for this purpose by the authors. Parents were asked to comment on the impact of the programs on their children and families, as well as the extent to which parents were actually involved. All parent interviews included a subscale of items taken directly from the pretest student self-report instrument. Thus, the way parents collectively defined different forms of child abuse were compared to their children's collective responses. All parents who agreed to be interviewed were interviewed.

Professionals

Most professional interviews ($n = 33$) were conducted by phone, although a few were conducted in person. Most professionals contacted were initially identified through administrators of the projects in the study as persons knowledgeable about their programs. (Because few child welfare workers and police were nominated, our sampling was constrained.) Interviews were with the project staff, high schools, police departments, and child welfare service units at county social service agencies. All instruments included the same definitional subscale used in the parent interview schedule.

A number of areas of inquiry were in these evaluations, including assessment of program impact on students, families, and institutions; assessment of program strengths and weaknesses; level of professional cooperation and preparation; and perceptions of program effectiveness. One particular focus of these schedules was to determine the extent of community involvement in the prevention programs as well as the level of cooperation between professionals in each school system and between various professionals and organizations in each community. Another focus was on the potential risks and benefits of CAPTA programs. A further set of questions asked what teaching approaches provide the optimum learning atmosphere for the purpose of teaching child abuse prevention in school settings. Interviews of professionals were begun immediately after parent interviews were completed. All professionals who agreed to be interviewed were interviewed.

Finally, during the data collection process, informal on-site observations were made of actual classroom teaching done by PPP staff in six classrooms. These observations were conducted by project staff.

Design of Interview Instruments

The design of each of the interview instrument followed a common process. In all cases, a review of the literature provided no instrument that was appropriate for the goals of these interviews: to provide additional insight into the effectiveness and impact of high school level child abuse prevention programs. Questions were generated from a consideration of these goals and the particular perspectives and roles of each target population. Thus, for example, although students, parents, and professionals were all asked about the strengths and weaknesses of the programs, the questions were aimed at the likely concerns of each group. The development of each instrument was completed and pilot-tested.

Definitional Survey

The responses of students, their parents, and various professionals to eleven items from the pretest questionnaire were collected. The purpose of the definitional survey was to compare the attitudes of students, parents, and professionals toward child abuse. All students who participated in the self-report pretests were included, as well as all parents and professionals who were interviewed. Each item asked the responder to choose to what degree a particular caretaker behavior should be considered abusive. All the items were Likert scaled, and are listed in table 3–9. The choices were strongly disagree, disagree, agree, and strongly agree. The responses were coded in the same way they had been coded on the pretest. All student responses were taken from the pretest self-report results. Parents and professionals were asked to respond to the items during their interviews.

In-State Survey

At the time that this study began, there was no accurate and updated description of the high school–level child abuse preven-

Table 3–9
Student Self-Report Items in Definitional Survey

Item Number	Item
14	Girl's parents emotionally abusing her.
21	Father physically abuses teen boy with belt.
22	Aunt sexually touches her teen nephew.
23	Teen has to miss school to watch siblings.
24	Teen boy hits girlfriend and apologizes.
25	Teen boy is turned on by young girl.
26	Teen boy in item 25 now touches girl.
27	Teen girl neglected; kicked out of house.
30	Date rape happens to girl at party.
33	Father emotionally abusive: always critical.
34	Father physically abusive: beats up son.

tion programs available. Such a description had to be completed before study sites were selected and the evaluation design and methods were constructed. An instrument was designed and mailed to all high school child abuse prevention programs in the state (see appendix B).

State by State Survey

During the course of the evaluation project, questions arose regarding how California high school–level CAPTA programs compare with similar prevention efforts in other states. Particular interest had to do with the relative priority given in other states to different age levels of students, different forms of child abuse, and alternative forms of prevention programs. An interview instrument was developed by the authors to collect this data (see appendix C). This instrument was developed after consulting with the literature, staff of the State of California Office of Child Abuse Prevention personnel, Office of Child Abuse Prevention, Regional Child Abuse Prevention Training Center staff, and the National Center for Child Abuse and Neglect. Professionals

($n = 22$) in other states were contacted, initially through a list of children's trust funds in over a dozen key states. Interviews were conducted by phone. When these administrators had little information, they were asked for the names of other administrators in their state. The information requested included the coordination and funding of adolescent abuse prevention programs; the existence of state mandates for adolescent abuse prevention programs; the level of cooperation between various prevention efforts and existing organizations; and state priorities for program curricula, target age groups, and types of abuse.

Family Life Programs

An effort was made to determine the extent to which family life education in the high schools already provides some of the curricula covered by CAPTA programs. Administrators in the California Department of Education and Family Life educators ($n = 5$) were interviewed, generally by phone, about state and community level policies. (Inquiries were also made with the administrators interviewed about the content of their family life classes.)

Human Subjects Protection

The rights and safety of human subjects were protected through the careful use of informed consent and confidentiality procedures. In general, the close monitoring of the effects of a program with sensitive content on a vulnerable population of young people offered potentially beneficial safeguards for both the students and parent participants. This study contributed to the improvement of the quality of child abuse prevention programs in schools by providing an analysis of the effectiveness and impact of CAPTA programs. Although this evaluation project was not designed to identify child abuse victims, two possible child abuse victims were identified through the process of data collection. Appropriate reporting of such cases to child protective services was completed by project staff. These reports are mandated by law and were intended in every case to benefit children and their families through the contact of appropriate child protective service agencies. Consent forms were designed for use with student questionnaires and student and parent interviews. Passive consent strategies were used with the questionnaires to ensure that a reasonable percentage of students would participate in the study. Active consent was obtained for parent and student interviews.

4
Study Results

Site selection efforts quickly clarified that neither the Office of Child Abuse Prevention nor the northern and southern training centers had comprehensive information on what was being taught in high school–level CAPTA programs. Little information existed on the methods used, the composition of the classes, and the qualifications of the presenters. A survey form was developed and mailed to all eighty-six primary prevention programs in the state: sixty programs responded, a return rate of 70 percent.

The results of the survey, shown in full in table 4–1, helped to describe current adolescent prevention programs in the state. Respondents were asked to indicate all topics covered in their programs and to identify two or three content areas that their programs emphasized. A total of twenty-seven areas of program content are listed in descending order of the content area most often cited. Acquaintance rape was most emphasized, followed, in order, by definitions and dynamics of child abuse, assertiveness training, self-empowerment, children's rights, and sexual abuse. These findings reflect the considerable influence of the CAP model in California.

Also interesting are the areas that receive little emphasis. A total of fourteen content areas were emphasized by less than three programs or were about 4 percent of all emphasized areas. These included physical abuse by adults and peers, emotional abuse, and parenting education. These areas also included five areas that were not emphasized by any programs: healthy sexuality, homosexuality and homophobia, self-identification as a possible abuser, sexual harassment, and stranger rape. Abduction

Table 4–1

Reports of High School–Level CAPTA Providers (n = 60) Regarding Their Program Content*

Content Area	Programs That Emphasize Content (in percent)	Programs That Cover Content But Do Not Emphasize Content (in percent)	Programs That Do Not Cover Content (in percent)
Acquaintance rape	30	68	2
Definitions and dynamics of child abuse	27	63	10
Assertiveness training	22	73	5
Self empowerment	22	62	17
Children's rights	18	70	12
Sexual abuse	15	85	0
Trust your feelings	13	78	8
Community resources	12	85	3
Decision making	12	67	22
Neglect	10	88	2
Communication skills	10	78	12
Incest	10	87	3
Self-esteem	10	75	15
Dealing with peer pressure	7	83	10
Physical abuse by adults	3	88	8
Physical abuse by peers	3	82	15
Touching (good vs. bad)	3	75	22
Emotional abuse	3	81	10
Parenting education	3	40	57
Sex roles	2	58	40
Self defense	2	58	40
Oppression	2	88	10
Helping a friend who is a victim or at risk	2	98	0
Stranger rape	0	90	10
Sexual harassment	0	57	43
Self-identification as a potential offender	0	47	53
Homosexuality/homophobia	0	48	52
Healthy sexuality	0	33	67

Mean number of content areas emphasized by program = 2.3

Mean number of content areas covered but not emphasized by each program = 19.6

*Because of rounding error all rows do not equal 100 percent was not identified for inclusion in the list or nominated as an "other" topic even though the law calls for its discussion.

Most PPPs provide programs with a total length of less than two hours, despite the rather high number of topics attempted by many programs. The six sites studied reported that they covered an average of about twenty-four of the twenty-seven items in the survey, which gives them theoretically about four minutes to cover each topic in a hundred-minute program. The average for all sixty programs was 196 topics and five minutes per topic. Of course, the topics do overlap and more than one topic can be covered at a time. About 90 percent of the programs were provided by PPP staff. Although 85 percent of the PPPs have parent meetings, the typical turnout is only three parents.

The Sample

A diverse and large ($n = 443$) group of high school students involved in the child abuse prevention programs were given self-report instruments. The number of boys and girls was almost identical (see table 4–2). The mean age of the students was 15.2. About a quarter of the students were Asian, about one-fifth were Hispanic, and approximately one-sixth were black. The remaining forty-three respondents were white, with 2 percent Native American Indians. Thus, black and Asian students were somewhat overrepresented, with white students somewhat underrepresented.

Almost one-fourth of the students lived with one parent. Mother's education was used as one approximation of social economic status; about one-sixth stated that their mother had less than a high school education. Almost one-fifth of the students indicated that their parent(s) were unemployed, which is higher than the current California unemployment rate. About two thirds of their parents who worked had white collar positions.

Pretest

The program and control groups were largely equivalent. ANOVAs on all scales showed no significant differences between

Table 4–2
Demographic Characteristics of Sample
(n = 443)

Sex	Percent
Male	50
Female	50
Age	
12	1
13	1
14	21
15	40
16	31
17	5
18	1
Ethnicity	
Asian American	25
Hispanic	20
Black	6
White	43
Native American	2
Other	4
Family Composition	
1 Parent	24
2 Parents	71
Other	5
Previous Class	
Human sexuality	69
Physical abuse	31
Sexual abuse	31
Protection from assault	20
Date rape	17
Emotional abuse	21
Child neglect	19
Family Income	
Parental employment	71
AFDC	4
Unemployment	2
Child support	1
SSI or social security	4
Workmen's compensation	6
Parents Working	
Professional or technical worker	23
Manager or business person	29
Clerical or sales worker	17
Skilled worker	14
Machine worker	6
Service worker	12

Table 4–2 (continued)

Sex	Percent
Laborer	12
Farm laborer	1
Armed services	2
Unknown	9
Mother's Education	
Less than 7th grade	5
Junior high school	3
Two years of high school	8
High school graduate	22
Some college or technical training	22
College graduate	18
Graduate school	8
Advanced professional training	8
Unknown	14

program and control groups in pretest scores (at the .05 level). In keeping, pretest frequencies (shown in table 4–3) are reported for the overall study sample. Percentage scores on the subscales are shown in table 4–4. Of all the scales, the highest scores of students prior to getting CAPTA programs is in the area of

Table 4–3
Percentage of Correct Scores On Each Scale for Pretest (n = 443)

	Mean	SD	Percent Correct
Date rape	15.4	2.51	76.9
Emotional abuse	21.3	2.94	78.8
Physical abuse	18.6	2.50	77.7
Sexual abuse	13.4	1.84	74.2
Assertiveness	15.7	2.40	87.0
Community resources	13.6	1.98	68.0
Neglect	9.2	1.65	76.9
Self-Identification	14.2	1.72	78.8
Skill intentions	26.5	4.40	71.6
Attitude	50.3	5.50	74.0
Knowledge	15.9	3.52	66.2
Summary	99.1	7.08	76.8

Table 4–4

Responses at Pretest*

Vignettes	N	Percent
1. You are tired of your mother yelling at you. What would you do?		
Turn on the television and ignore her.	54	12
Tell her calmly but firmly that you don't like her yelling at you.	150	34
Scream at your mother and slam the door.	85	19
Let her yell and do what she tells you to do.	149	35
2. John's new stepfather becomes angry and violent when he drinks. Last weekend, the stepfather slapped John's mother and threatened John. What should John do?		
Nothing, because the stepfather usually apologizes after he is sober again.	4	1
Hide the alcohol in the house or pour it down the drain.	15	3
Try to talk with his mother about the problem. If she won't do anything about it, then he may have to go talk to someone else for help.	352	80
John should tell his stepfather to leave his mother alone. If he doesn't listen, he should force him out of the house.	68	16
3. A teenage girl has an older brother who kept trying to get her alone. One evening he put his hand up her blouse. He quickly left the room when he heard his mother call him.		
The girl shouldn't tell anyone because her brother could get in a lot of trouble.	2	1
She should just forget it because it probably won't happen again.	3	1
She should tell him to stop.	82	18
She should tell him to stop and find someone who can help her.	338	77
She should get her boyfriend to beat her brother up.	16	4
4. Jim is a seventeen-year-old boy who has few friends his own age. Lately he has been wanting to have sex with a girl he knows who is only nine. What should he do?		
Nothing because he's done nothing wrong.	34	8

Table 4–4 (continued)

Vignettes	N	Percent
Try not to think about it because the feelings will go away.	93	21
Keep quiet since he will get in trouble if he says anything.	30	7
Talk to an adult about it.	281	64
5. Your mother and father are always fighting with each other. During the last year, the fighting has grown worse, and they are now yelling at you more, too. You are feeling very upset. What should you do?		
Get used to it, because it won't change.	17	4
Tell your parents how you feel, or talk to someone else about your problem.	263	60
Stay out of their way as much as you can.	57	13
Try to get your parents to stop fighting, and try to keep everything as calm at home as possible.	102	23
6. You are an eighteen-year-old girl who lives alone with your three-month-old baby. It seems like the baby cries constantly, and nothing you do seems to help. Last night you started to really feel like hitting your baby, and your anger scared you. What should you do?		
Try to find someone to talk to because you need some help and understanding right now.	360	82
Deal with it on your own, because that's how you learn to be a good parent.	51	12
You should not allow your baby to cry so much because that much is crying not normal.	8	2
You should ignore the crying, regardless of how long it goes on.	22	5
7. John is a fourteen-year-old who is very close to his cousin, Martin, who is twenty. Martin told John that the best way for John to learn about sex would be for the two of them to play with each other's genitals. John does not want to. What should John do?		
Avoid Martin and act as if nothing happened.	73	17
Talk with an adult about what happened.	265	65

(continued)

Table 4–4 (continued)

Vignettes	N	Percent
Do a few things with Martin, and then tell Martin to leave him alone.	9	2
Tell Martin he'll beat him up if he even says that again.	75	17
8. Name two places you could call if you had been abused. (multiple responses)		
Police	182	20
CPS	72	8
Professional Agency	90	10
School	21	2
Family	112	13
Friend	69	8
Women's shelter	5	1
Other	55	6
Don't know/blank	278	32
9. Who are two people you know that you could go to if you had been abused (do *not* give their actual names)? (multiple response)		
Parent/guardian	165	19
Other family	239	27
Professional	50	6
Friend (peer)	235	27
Friend (adult)	27	3
Unspecified	38	4
Other	30	3
Don't know/blank	100	11
10. If a friend told me that her stepfather had felt her breasts, I would: (multiple response)		
Tell her to say NO	24	5
Tell professional/cops	42	10
Tell parent/guardian	100	23
Tell someone/get help	113	26
Protect self/defense	4	1
Violent response	14	3
Passive response	10	2
Keep telling until helped	2	1

Table 4–4 (continued)

Vignettes	N	Percent
Don't give advice/take responsibility	46	10
Other	53	12
Don't know/blank	35	8
11. Your sister's boyfriend is pressuring her to have sex. She likes him but is not ready to have sex. What are two things you would tell her to do? (multiple response)		
Say NO/talk	380	43
Tell someone	48	5
Break up	172	19
Violent response	42	5
Passive response	42	5
Other	132	15
Don't know/blank	98	22
12. In the past, John has hit his girlfriend when he was angry. Name two things he could do to stop hurting her when he gets angry again. (multiple response)		
Talk to her	92	10
Alternative expression of anger, destructive	50	6
Alternative expression of anger, nondestructive	78	9
Self-awareness (control)	155	16
Time out	162	18
Get help	113	13
Other	99	11
Don't know/blank	135	15
13. Bob has been baby-sitting a one-year-old girl for about four months. Over that time, she has not gained any weight, and looks very quiet and tired most of the time. What should Bob do? (multiple response)		
Talk to baby's parent	191	43
Doctor	91	21
Professional	13	3
Talk with his family/friend	30	7
Avoid/deny	16	4

(continued)

Table 4–4 (continued)

Vignettes	N	Percent
Other	60	14
Don't know/blank	41	9

Vignettes	M	SD
14. If a girl's parents always tell her that she's no good and don't ever let her talk with friends, they are emotionally abusing her.**	3.3	.74
15. If a guy wants sex, he has to pressure a girl.	1.7	.69
16. If a boy is sexually abused by a man, the boy will probably become gay (homosexual).	2.0	.74
17. It's hard for girls to say what they really feel about having sex.	2.6	.78
18. It's difficult for boys to be sensitive and caring with girls when they're expected to be tough and in charge.	2.3	.84
19. It's fine for a girl to say what she wants, but the guy should have the final say.	1.7	.76
20. If a teenager was abused as a child, there is no point in reporting because it was too long ago.	1.7	.76
21. This last year, a father hit his son three times with a belt. Each time he left marks on his son. This is abuse.**	3.1	.75
22. A forty-year-old aunt decides she wants to have sex with her sixteen-year-old nephew. She touches him in a way that turns him on, and then she has sex with him. This is abuse.**	2.9	.83
23. Mary often has to miss school because her parents make her take care of her brothers and sisters. This is abuse.**	2.9	.82
24. One night after a party, a boy punches his girlfriend. He apologizes and says it won't happen again. This is abuse.**	3.0	.80
25. A teenager is baby-sitting a three-year-old girl. He gets turned on when he helps her change into her pajamas. This is abuse.**	2.4	.81
26. The same boy (in the last question) puts his hand down the girl's pajama bottoms. This is abuse.**	3.4	.63
27. A fifteen-year-old girl is supposed to be home by 12:00 A.M., but doesn't get home until 3:00 A.M. The next morning her parents tell her to pack		

Table 4-4 (continued)

Vignettes	N	Percent
some things and not come home until she can live by their rules. This is a case of neglect.**	2.0	.70
28. Where can this girl go if she doesn't have friends or relatives to turn to?		
Police	49	11
CPS	11	3
Professional/hotline	79	18
School	10	2
Family	5	1
Friend	9	2
Shelter/foster home	152	35
Other (streets)	29	7
Don't know/blank	97	22
29. A teenager is more likely to be abused by a stranger than by someone they know.	2.0	.70
30. Bill got together with Lisa at a party. Lisa enjoyed kissing him, but got nervous when he started touching her below the waist. She started to pull away, but Bill thought she was just being a tease and continued. Lisa became frightened and started to struggle. Bill seemed so much stronger. She couldn't stop him from having sex with her. This is case of rape.**	3.2	.79
31. Lisa was partly to blame because she led him on.	2.4	.81
32. Lisa must have liked it because she didn't make him stop.	2.0	.86
33. Jack's father always tells him that he will never amount to anything because he's lazy snd stupid. This is emotional abuse even though his father is sometimes very nice to him.**	3.0	.63
34. John had an accident and wrecked his father's car. When his father found out, he lost his temper and beat up John. This is child abuse even though John thought he deserved it.**	3.0	.81

*The most desired responses are underlined.

**Items in eleven-item definitional survey. Due to rounding and multiple response items, percentages may not equal 100.

assertiveness, with a score of 87 percent correct. The lowest score (67 percent) was in knowledge of community resources. Other subscale scores were closely clustered together between 74 and 79 percent correct. There is no way to tell the degree to which the differences between these scores are due to certain items being easier, differences between how well students were prepared in certain areas, or other factors (such as item validity).

Pretest results, when considered item by item, provided insight into what items were appropriately difficult at the pretest level, and which items may have to be redesigned or replaced in future studies. For example, over 80 percent of the students chose the most desired response to item 2 on the pretest. This skewed distribution of scores suggests that most students have already mastered the concept of a physically abusive and violent stepfather. Only 12 percent of the students chose the most desired response regarding whether it is neglectful for parents to force a girl to miss school so she can baby-sit, however, and the responses are quite normally distributed.

The relationship between characteristics and pretest scores was assessed through analysis of variance (see appendix D for the complete breakdown). Pretest scores were compared for four key student characteristics: previous child maltreatment class experience, mother's level of education, student ethnicity, and student sex. A fifth factor used in interaction with the other variables was group status: whether the student was in the program or control group. Each of the nine scales were used as dependent variables, assessed at each of the three assessment periods: pretest, posttest, and follow-up. Girls scored significantly (.05 level) higher than boys on all scales except for neglect and physical abuse (in which girls still outscored boys). Overall, girls scored much higher than boys (.001 level). Significant (.05 level) differences were found between ethnic groups in several scales: community resources, self-identification, neglect, emotional abuse, physical abuse, and the summary scale. When their mothers had less than a high school education, students scored significantly (.05 level) lower in all scales except for date rape and sexual abuse. Asian and Hispanic students had the lowest pretest scores, and Blacks the highest scores on the summary scale.

Family characteristics and prior class experience were related to summary scores. The summary scale score was found to be significantly correlated $(r=.23;$ $p<.001)$ with mother's education; students with more educated mothers had higher scores. Students also had significantly higher scores when they attended previous child maltreatment classes $(r=.18;$ $p<.001)$.

Posttest

In general, posttest results showed that students who received the program made positive, and often statistically significant changes in knowledge, attitudes, and intentions. Individual items provided indications of how well various topics were learned. Because the tests of thirty-four items increase the likely chance of findings, the alpha level was set at .03. Program group students scored significantly higher than control group students on five items, including those with content in such areas as psychological maltreatment by a parent (item 1), sexual molestation of a boy (item 7), community resources (items 9 and 11), and knowledge that most abuse is committed by people you know (item 29) (see table 4–5). Students learn less about substance abuse in the family (item 2), sibling molestation (item 3), parenting skills (item 6), and neglect (item 27).

Analysis of posttest scales scores showed higher scores for program group students over control group students in all areas (see table 4–6) and significantly higher scores for program group students on seven scales: sexual abuse, assertiveness, community resources, neglect, intended skills, knowledge, and all. However, program membership explained little of the overall variance (R^2 values were generally under .05).

ANOVA was also used to test the effects of sex, ethnicity, and mother's education on improvements between pretest and posttest. No significant effect was found between these variables and any scale gain score.

The percentage of respondents who answered each response on each vignette at posttest and responded to the open-ended items related to community resources and behavioral intentions is shown in table 4–7. Percentage change in responses is also

Table 4–5
Differences of First Posttest Item Scores by Group

		Program Group		Control Group	
		n	Mean	n	Mean
1. Psychological abuse	245	2.48	191	2.28	2.90*
2. Physical abuse	246	2.72	191	2.74	−0.44
3. Sibling molestation	244	2.90	196	2.90	−0.01
4. Self-Identification	244	2.57	195	2.49	1.06
5. Psychological abuse	246	2.59	196	2.43	2.12
6. Parenting skills	247	2.75	196	2.78	−0.53
7. Sexual molestation	244	2.62	196	2.43	2.70*
8. Resources	181	3.34	124	3.27	0.84
9. Resources	215	2.27	173	2.16	2.38*
10. Molestation	219	1.80	176	1.70	0.50
11. Resources	215	3.25	169	3.00	3.64*
12. Peer abuse	143	3.83	102	3.84	−0.11
13. Neglect	199	2.78	157	2.78	0.06
14. Psychological abuse	246	3.43	194	3.37	0.96
15. Acquaintance rape	244	3.35	195	3.26	1.44
16. Abuse of males	241	3.15	195	3.02	1.99
17. Acquaintance rape	245	2.47	195	2.53	−0.71
18. Acquaintance rape	246	2.72	193	2.81	−1.10
19. Acquaintance rape	246	3.30	194	3.25	0.68
20. Reporting	247	3.34	194	3.22	1.94
21. Physical abuse	246	3.17	192	3.11	0.65
22. Abuse of males	244	2.95	193	2.83	1.63
23. Neglect	244	2.82	194	2.78	0.55
24. Peer abuse	245	3.10	191	2.96	1.87
25. Sexual abuse	245	2.67	196	2.62	0.61
26. Sexual abuse	246	3.37	194	3.35	0.46
27. Neglect	244	2.92	195	2.94	−0.23
28. Resources	206	3.70	138	3.65	0.48
29. Know abusers	244	3.12	196	2.90	3.64*
30. Acquaintance rape	245	3.16	196	3.05	1.61
31. Acquaintance rape	245	2.74	196	2.70	0.49
32. Acquaintance rape	241	3.11	195	3.04	0.95
33. Psychological abuse	242	3.05	195	3.03	0.38
34. Physical abuse	242	3.00	193	3.10	−1.31

*Significant at the .03 level

Table 4–6
Differences of Posttest Scale Scores by Group (n = 405)

	Program Mean	Control Mean	F
Date rape	15.75	15.32	2.79
Emotional abuse	21.94	21.47	2.91
Physical abuse	18.73	18.59	.31
Sexual abuse	13.52	12.91	6.69**
Assertiveness	16.25	15.75	4.20*
Community resources	11.70	10.53	9.55**
Neglect	8.32	7.77	4.79*
Self-Identification	14.21	13.82	2.98
Skill Intentions	29.06	27.46	7.12**
Attitude	52.24	51.52	0.88
Knowledge	17.95	16.18	17.93***
Summary	97.58	93.74	13.76***

*$P < .05$
**$P < .01$
***$P < .001$

shown and indicates the largest changes were increases in item 1 of the likelihood of telling a parent that you don't like her yelling at you (rather than yelling back or saying nothing and just doing as told) and in items 10 and 11, which show greater knowledge of when and where to get help.

Effect Sizes

Because statistical significance is an imperfect indicator of the value of differences between groups, *effect sizes* help estimate the meaningfulness of the improvements in scores (Wolf 1986) (see table 4–8). Three types of effect sizes were computed. The first (*d*) is the difference between the mean scores of two groups divided by the standard deviation of the groups; *d* is in standard deviation units. According to accepted guidelines (Cohen 1977), nine scales showed small effects (below .35), and two scales showed moderate effects (between .35 and .50). None showed large effects. Acquaintance rape's effect size of .15 indicates that

Table 4–7
Responses at Posttest and Change from Pretest*

Vignettes	N	Percent	Percent Change
1. You are tired of your mother yelling at you. What would you do?			
Turn on the television and ignore her.	40	9	− 3
Tell her calmly but firmly that you don't like her yelling at you.	231	53	+ 19
Scream at your mother and slam the door.	61	14	− 5
Let her yell and do what she tells you to do.	104	24	− 11
2. John's new stepfather becomes angry and violent when he drinks. Last weekend, the stepfather slapped John's mother and threatened John. What should John do?			
Nothing, because the stepfather usually apologizes after he is sober again.	3	1	0
Hide the alcohol in the house or pour it down the drain.	16	4	+ 1
Try to talk with his mother about the problem. If she won't do anything about it, then he may have to go talk to someone else for help.	368	84	+ 4
John should tell his stepfather to leave his mother alone. If he doesn't listen, he should force him out of the house.	50	11	− 5
3. A teenage girl has an older brother who kept trying to get her alone. One evening he put his hand up her blouse. He quickly left the room when he heard his mother call him.			
The girl shouldn't tell anyone because her brother could get in a lot of trouble.	1	1	0
She should just forget it because it probably won't happen again.	6	1	0
She should tell him to stop.	75	18	− 1
She should tell him to stop and find someone who can help her.	339	77	0
She should get her boyfriend to beat her brother up.	19	4	0
4. Jim is a seventeen-year-old boy who has few friends his own age. Lately he has been wanting to have sex with a girl he knows who is only nine. What should he do?			
Nothing because he's done nothing wrong.	28	6	− 2
Try not to think about it because the feelings will go away.	79	18	− 3

Table 4–7 (continued)

Vignettes	N	Percent	Percent Change
Keep quiet because he will get in trouble if he says anything.	18	4	−3
Talk to an adult about it.	315	72	+8
5. Your mother and father are always fighting with each other. During the last year, the fighting has grown worse, and they are now yelling at you more, too. You are feeling very upset. What should you do?			
Get used to it, because it won't change.	14	3	+1
Tell your perents how you feel, or talk to someone else about your problem.	306	69	+9
Stay out of their way as much as you can.	44	10	−3
Try to get your parents to stop fighting, and try to keep everything as calm at home as possible.	78	18	−5
6. You are an eighteen-year-old girl who lives alone with your three-month-old baby. It seems like the baby cries constantly, and nothing you do seems to help. Last night you started to really feel like hitting your baby, and your anger scared you. What should you do?			
Try to find someone to talk to because you need some help and understanding right now.	358	81	−1
Deal with it on your own, because that's how you learn to be a good parent.	48	11	−1
You should not allow your baby to cry so much because that much crying is not normal.	21	5	+3
You should ignore the crying, regardless of how long it goes on.	16	4	−1
7. John is a fourteen-year-old who is very close to his cousin, Martin, who is twenty. Martin told John that the best way for John to learn about sex would be for the two of them to play with each other's genitals. John does not want to. What should John do?			
Avoid Martin and act as if nothing happened.	56	13	−3
Talk with an adult about what happened.	307	70	+5
Do a few things with Martin, and then tell Martin to leave him alone.	6	1	−1
Tell Martin he'll beat him up if he even says that again.	71	16	−1

(continued)

Table 4–7 (continued)

Vignettes	N	Percent	Percent Change
Knowledge			
8. Name two places you could call if you had been abused.			
Police	172	20	0
CPS	91	10	+2
Professional Agency	147	17	+7
School	21	2	0
Family	90	10	−3
Friend	71	8	0
Women's shelter	25	3	+2
Other	65	7	+1
Don't know/blank	204	23	−9
9. Who are two people you know that you could go to if you had been abused (do *not* give their actual names)?			
Parent/guardian	166	44	+25
Other family	209	24	−3
Professional	87	10	+4
Friend (peer)	230	26	−1
Friend (adult)	28	3	0
Unspecified	41	5	+1
Other	39	4	+1
Don't know/blank	82	9	−2
10. If a friend told me that her stepfather had felt her breasts, I would:			
Tell her to say NO	28	6	+1
Tell professional/cops	45	10	0
Tell parent/guardian	94	21	−2
Tell someone/get help	169	38	+12
Protect self/defense	4	1	0
Violent response	10	2	−1
Passive response	8	2	0
Keep telling until helped	2	1	0
Don't give advice/take responsibility	33	8	−2
Other	25	6	−6
Don't know/blank	21	5	−3

Table 4–7 (continued)

Vignettes	N	Percent	Percent Change
11. Your sister's boyfriend is pressuring her to have sex. She likes him but is not ready to have sex. What are two things you would tell her to do?			
Say NO/talk	400	45	+2
Tell someone	61	7	+2
Break up	173	17	−2
Violent response	16	2	−3
Passive response	46	5	0
Other	121	14	−1
Don't know/blank	72	8	−14
12. In the past, John has hit his girlfriend when he was angry. name two things he could do to stop hurting her when he gets angry again.			
Talk to her	92	10	0
Alternative expression of anger, destructive	47	5	−1
Alternative expression of anger, nondestructive	65	7	−2
Self-awareness (control)	163	18	+2
Time out	154	18	0
Get help	156	17	−4
Other	93	11	0
Don't know/blank	117	13	−2
13. Bob has been baby-sitting a one-year-old girl for about four months. Over that time, she has not gained any weight, and looks very quiet and tired most of the time. What should Bob do?			
Talk to baby's parent	186	42	−1
Doctor	93	21	0
Professional	28	6	+3
Talk with his family/friend	39	9	+2
Other	63	14	0
14. If a girl's parents always tell her that she's no good and don't ever let her talk with friends, they are emotionally abusing her.	3.4	.70	+.1
15. If a guy wants sex, he has to pressure a girl.	1.7	.70	0

(*continued*)

Table 4–7 (continued)

Vignettes	N	Percent	Percent Change
16. If a boy is sexually abused by a man, the boy will probably become gay (homosexual).	1.9	.70	− .1
17. It's hard for girls to say what they really feel about having sex.	2.5	.81	− .1
18. It's difficult for boys to be sensitive and caring with girls when they're expected to be tough and in charge.	2.2	.84	− .1
19. It's fine for a girl to say what she wants, but the guy should have the final say.	1.7	.73	0
20. If a teenager was abused as a child, there is no point in reporting because it was too long ago.	1.7	.66	0
21. This last year, a father hit his son three times with a belt. Each time he left marks on his son. This is abuse.	3.1	.80	0
22. A forty-year-old aunt decides she wants to have sex with her sixteen-year-old nephew. She touches him in a way that turns him on, and then she has sex with him. This is abuse.	2.9	.84	0
23. Mary often has to miss school because her parents make her take care of her brothers and sisters. This is abuse.	2.8	.78	− .1
24. One night after a party, a boy punches his girlfriend. He apologizes and says it won't happen again. This is abuse.	3.0	.77	0
25. A teenager is baby-sitting a three-year-old girl. He gets turned on when he helps her change into her pajamas. This is abuse.	2.4	.74	0
26. The same boy (in the last question) puts his hand down the girl's pajama bottoms. This is abuse.	3.4	.65	0
27. A fifteen-year-old girl is supposed to be home by 12:00 A.M., but doesn't get home until 3:00 A.M. The next morning her parents tell her to pack some things and not come home until she can live by their rules. This is a case of neglect.	2.9	.74	+ .9
28. Where can this girl go if she doesn't have friends or relatives to turn to?			
Police	49	11	0
CPS	11	3	0
Professional/hotline	79	18	0

Table 4–7 (continued)

Vignettes	N	Percent	Percent Change
School	10	2	0
Family	5	1	0
Friend	9	2	0
Shelter/foster home	152	35	0
Other (streets)	29	7	0
Don't know/blank	97	22	0
29. A teenager is more likely to be abused by a stranger than someone they know.	2.0	.66	0
30. Bill got together with Lisa at a party. Lisa enjoyed kissing him, but got nervous when he started touching her below the waist. She started to pull away, but Bill thought she was just being a tease and continued. Lisa became frightened and started to struggle. Bill seemed so much stronger. She couldn't stop him from having sex with her. This is a case of rape.	3.1	.77	−.1
31. Lisa was partly to blame because she led him on.	2.3	.83	−.1
32. Lisa must have liked it becawse she didn't make him stop.		.74	.1
33. Jack's father always tells him that he will never amount to anything because he's lazy and stupid. This is emotional abuse even though his father is sometimes very nice to him.	3.0	.66	0
34. John had an accident and wrecked his father's car. When his father found out, he lost his temper and beat up John. This is child abuse even though John thought he deserved it.	3.0	.81	0

*The most desired responses are underlined; on multiple choice items, percentages may not sum to 100 because of rounding error and change scores may not sum to zero because of rounding error. On multiple response items, change scores may not sum to zero because the number of responses from pretest to posttest varies.

the average student receiving the curriculum would have a score that is .15 standard deviations higher than a student who did not take the class; his or her score would go from the fiftieth percentile to the fifty-ninth. The two other effect sizes show the difference in the percent of students who improved in the program group compared with the percent who improved in the

Table 4–8
Effect Sizes of Program at Posttest (n = 443)

Scale	d		ES1** (in percent)	ES2*** (in percent)
Date rape	0.15		10.56	18.66
Emotional abuse	0.13		8.59	9.70
Physical abuse	0.06		14.35	7.75
Sexual abuse	0.16		17.05	13.88
Assertiveness	0.28		8.90	13.57
Community resources		0.25	14.21	09.09
Neglect	0.20		4.59	4.37
Self-Identification	0.13		9.26	2.46
Skill intentions	0.27		8.90	13.57
Attitude	0.19		16.22	10.13
Knowledge	0.41		21.40	18.25
All		0.37	23.10	16.95

*d = (mean of program group) minus (mean of control group) divided by (SD of control)

**ES1 = (number improved in program group divided by total number in program group) minus (number
improved in control group divided by total number in control group)

***ES2 = (number improved at least 10 percent in program group divided by total number in program group) minus (number improved at least 10 percent in control group divided by total number in control group)

control group (ES1) and the difference in the percent of students who improved at least 10 percent in the program versus control group. These are shown in table 4–8. Approximately 23 percent more students improved in the program group than in the control group. That is, three of four students did not learn any more than they would have if they had not taken the class. About 17 percent more program group students had at least a 10 percent improvement. Only one of six students who received the program learned 10 percent more than the typical student who never took the class. No method of computing effect sizes shows large effects.

The use of ANOVA on the gain in scores from pretest to posttest helps estimate posttest differences above and beyond pretest differences. As can be seen in table 4–9, program group

Table 4–9

Differences between Mean Gain Scores from Pretest to Posttest

	N	Program	Control	F
Date rape	374	0.27	− 0.08	3.47
Emotional abuse	374	0.71	0.26	4.24*
Physical abuse	374	0.16	− 0.15	1.75
Sexual abuse	374	0.45	− 0.14	10.34***
Assertiveness	374	0.59	0.15	5.60*
Community resources	358	1.56	0.63	7.94**
Neglect	358	0.65	0.49	0.38
Self-Identification	358	0.50	0.18	2.09
All	358		4.78	1.36	23.41***
Skill intentions	358	1.60	0.77	4.57*
Attitude	358	1.62	0.34	9.69**
Knowledge	358	1.56	0.25	20.18***

*p < .05
**p < .01
***p < .001

students scored significantly (at least .05 level) higher than control group students in eight of the twelve scales. ANOVA was also used to test the effects of sex, ethnicity, and mother's education on initial gains (table 4–9). Although, as described above, some of these variables did have an effect on pretest and posttest scores, no significant effect was found on any scale gain score.

The percentage of total score for each scale at posttest was calculated for the program and control group (see table 4–10). Mean values of item and scale scores in the various tables will differ somewhat because the sample size differs slightly with each calculation.

Overall results of the ANOVA techniques showed significant differences in student scores with group status, student sex, student ethnicity, and to a lesser extent, mother's education. In all subscale scores, girls scored higher than boys. Girls scored significantly (.05 level) higher than boys in the community resources, self-identification, date rape, emotional abuse, sexual abuse, assertiveness, and overall scales. Significant (.05) differences were also found between ethnic groupings in the community re-

Table 4–10
Percentage of Total Score Possible at Posttest

| | Program | | Control | | |
	Mean	Percent	Mean Percent	Difference	
Date rape	15.73	78.6	15.31	76.6	2.0
Psychological abuse	21.85	80.9	21.51	79.7	1.2
Physical abuse	18.71	78.0	18.57	77.4	0.6
Sexual abuse	13.73	76.3	13.24	73.6	2.7
Assertiveness	16.18	89.9	15.76	87.6	2.3
Community resources	13.90	69.5	13.64	68.2	1.3
Neglect	9.48	79.0	9.44	78.7	0.3
Self-Identification	14.67	81.5	14.45	80.3	1.2
Skill intentions	28.75	77.7	27.67	74.8	2.9
Attitude	52.37	77.0	52.09	76.6	0.4
Knowledge	17.34	72.2	16.70	69.6	2.6
All	101.93	79.0	98.67	76.5	3.5

sources, neglect, emotional abuse, and overall scales. Generally, Asian students had the lowest scores. Students who had mothers with at least a high school education scored significantly (.05 level) higher in the community resources and overall scales. Prior class experience made no significant difference on any scale.

Relationships of specific demographic (independent) variables with initial gain scores were estimated using ANOVA. Only one variable was found to have close to a significant ($p<.052$) effect on gain scores of the summary scale from pretest to posttest—students with mothers with higher education tended to have higher gain scores. Length of class was not found to be related with gain scores. No particular ethnic group had a significant relationship with gain scores.

Follow-up

The key comparisons to be made with follow-up data is that between program group posttest scores and program group follow-up scores, which are essentially measures of retention. Such comparisons were made with individual items; the alpha level was again set at .03.

Follow-up scores were significantly higher (.03 level) than posttest scores for four items (shown in sixth column in table 4–11). These items included content on how a girl might stand up to a boyfriend who is pressuring her (11), boys feeling comfortable about being sensitive to girls (18), a girl's right to say no to a boy (19), and the physical abuse of a boy by his father (34). Item differences between all three observations are shown in table 4–11. (The mean values given in the first three columns differ slightly from previous tables as the number of cases vary when doing comparisons between each pair of observations.)

Individual items and responses are shown in table 4–12. The table also shows percentage change in responses from pretest. Items that showed large changes at posttest typically showed even greater gains by follow-up. For example, the test typically showed even greater gains by follow-up. The percentage of students who responded to item 1 of calmly but firmly telling a parent that you don't like to be yelled at increased another 6 percent from posttest. Calling CPS if you had been abused (item 8) increased only 2 percent from pretest to posttest but went up another 11 percent by follow-up. The percentage that did not know what to do had declined by 15 percent from pretest to posttest. All together, the three most favorable responses to item 12 (your sister's boyfriend is pressuring her to have sex) increased an average of 12 percent by follow-up.

Using ANOVA (see table 4–13), scale scores were compared between posttest and follow-up for the program group. Follow-up scores were significantly (at least .05 level) higher than posttest scores in eight scales. Again, R^2 values in all scales were less than .05.

In table 4–14, the mean scale scores of program group students are compared across all three observations: pretest, posttest, and follow-up. The mean values given in the first three columns vary slightly as the number of cases vary when doing comparisons between each pair of observations.

The percentage of total possible scale scores for program group students at all three observations can also be compared

Table 4–11
Differences between Item Scores for Program Group**

M	Pretest (1) SD	Posttest (2) M	SD	Follow-up (3) M	SD	t Value 1 to 2	t Value 2 to 3	t Value 1 to 3
1 2.14	.69	2.54	.66	2.48	.69	7.07*	−0.73	4.49*
2 2.62	.76	2.80	.56	2.86	.50	2.17	1.24	2.50*
3 2.93	.33	2.95	.30	2.97	.25	1.51	0.45	0.24
4 2.42	.81	2.59	.75	2.67	.71	2.80*	1.32	3.32*
5 2.38	.83	2.59	.74	2.64	.73	3.37*	0.62	2.53*
6 2.80	.45	2.75	.56	2.83	.44	1.33	1.52	0.35
7 2.49	.75	2.72	.64	2.75	.59	2.97*	0.55	2.32*
8 2.86	.89	2.80	1.20	3.10	.86	3.64*	−1.05	3.30*
9 2.05	.48	2.05	.71	2.05	.84	3.87*	−0.11	1.49
10 1.66	.77	1.77	2.73	1.73	2.90	0.92	−0.18	1.18
11 2.96	.78	2.96	.98	3.30	1.22	2.00	3.14**	2.98*
12 3.06	.98	2.89	1.52	3.12	1.78	1.96	1.47	1.30
13 2.66	.96	2.27	1.35	2.52	1.41	1.85	2.04	0.98
14 3.28	.88	3.41	.71	3.56	.80	2.46*	1.96	3.22*
16 3.02	.69	3.21	.60	3.20	.76	2.81*	−0.12	2.09
17 2.46	.82	2.51	.79	1.59	.86	0.33	1.02	1.35
18 2.70	.82	2.74	.81	2.94	1.03	0.21	2.31*	2.10
19 3.28	.77	3.35	.69	3.52	.77	0.50	2.51*	1.62
20 3.25	.64	3.40	.63	3.41	.76	2.27*	0.23	2.14
21 3.08	.86	3.21	.85	3.27	.91	1.47	0.77	1.34
22 2.81	.92	2.97	.81	3.08	.88	2.45*	1.50	3.23*
23 2.60	.79	2.85	.81	2.88	.85	4.88*	0.42	3.32*
24 3.00	.80	3.12	.76	3.19	.73	1.83	1.08	1.94
25 2.56	.76	2.72	.71	2.66	.76	2.22*	−0.93	1.09
26 3.39	.63	3.37	.69	3.48	.65	0.36	2.01	1.73
27 2.94	.76	2.95	.76	3.00	.90	0.23	0.69	0.96
28 3.54	1.01	3.20	1.55	3.77	.77	3.14*	−0.69	0.60
29 3.00	.68	3.13	.60	3.20	.73	2.53*	1.08	3.49*
30 3.24	.72	3.25	.74	3.29	.91	1.46	0.58	0.65
31 2.60	.78	2.84	.83	2.90	.82	3.00*	0.86	2.75*
32 2.99	.75	3.16	.69	3.32	.82	2.39*	2.26	2.91*
33 2.96	.66	3.03	.68	3.12	.73	1.97	1.33	2.88*
34 2.92	.92	3.09	.80	3.30	.91	1.32	2.53*	3.86*

*p < .03
**n varies from 97 to 132 because of missing cases

Table 4–12

*Responses at Follow-up and Change from Pretest**

Vignettes	N	Percent	Percent Change
1. You are tired of your mother yelling at you. What would you do?			
Turn on the television and ignore her.	19	8	−4
Tell her calmly but firmly that you don't like her yelling at you.	132	55	+21
Scream at your mother and slam the door.	39	16	−3
Let her yell and do what she tells you to do.	50	21	−14
2. John's new stepfather becomes angry and violent when he drinks. Last weekend, the stepfather slapped John's mother and threatened John. What should John do?			
Nothing, because the stepfather usually apologizes after he is sober again.	0	0	−1
Hide the alcohol in the house or pour it down the drain.	4	2	−1
Try to talk with his mother about the problem. If she won't do anything about it, then he may have to go talk to someone else for help.	216	90	+10
John should tell his stepfather to leave his mother alone. If he doesn't listen, he should force him out of the house.	20	8	−8
3. A teenage girl has an older brother who kept trying to get her alone. One evening he put his hand up her blouse. He quickly left the room when he heard his mother call him.			
The girl shouldn't tell anyone because her brother could get in a lot of trouble.	2	1	0
She should just forget it because it probably won't happen again.	3	1	0
She should tell him to stop.	27	11	−7
She should tell him to stop and find someone who can help her.	205	84	+7
She should get her boyfriend to beat her brother up.	6	3	−1
4. Jim is a seventeen-year-old boy who has few friends his own age. Lately he has been			

(*continued*)

Table 4–12 (continued)

Vignettes	N	Percent	Percent Change
wanting to have sex with a girl he knows who is only nine. What should he do?			
Nothing because he's done nothing wrong.	9	4	−4
Try not to think about it because the feelings will go away.	3	17	−4
Keep quiet because he will get in trouble if he says anything.	8	3	−4
Talk to an adult about it.	187	77	+13
5. Your mother and father are always fighting with each other. During the last year, the fighting has grown worse, and they are now yelling at you more, too. You are feeling very upset. What should you do?			
Get used to it, because it won't change.	2	1	−3
Tell your perents how you feel, or talk to someone else about your problem.	187	77	+17
Stay out of their way as much as you can.	18	7	−6
Try to get your parents to stop fighting, and try to keep everything as calm at home as possible.	36	15	−8
6. You are an eighteen-year-old girl who lives alone with your three-month-old baby. It seems like the baby cries constantly, and nothing you do seems to help. Last night you started to really feel like hitting your baby, and your anger scared you. What should you do?			
Try to find someone to talk to because you need some help and understanding right now.	210	86	+4
Deal with it on your own, because that's how you learn to be a good parent.	19	8	−4
You should not allow your baby to cry so much because that much crying is not normal.	4	2	0
You should ignore the crying, regardless of how long it goes on.	11	5	0
7. John is a fourteen year old who is very close to his cousin, Martin, who is twenty. Martin told John that the best way for John to learn			

Table 4–12 (continued)

Vignettes	N	Percent	Percent Change
about sex would be for the two of them to play with each other's genitals. John does not want to. What should John do?			
Avoid Martin and act as if nothing happened.	27	11	−6
Talk with an adult about what happened.	181	75	+10
Do a few things with Martin, and then tell Martin to leave him alone.	0	0	−2
Tell Martin he'll beat him up if he even says that again.	35	14	−3
Knowledge			
8. Name two places you could call if you had been abused.			
Police	96	19	−1
CPS	103	21	+13
Professional Agency	57	11	+1
School	8	2	0
Family	66	14	+1
Friend	57	12	+4
Women's shelter	7	2	+1
Other	6	1	−5
Don't know/blank	86	17	−15
9. Who are two people you know that you could go to if you had been abused (do *not* give their actual names)?			
Parent/guardian	113	23	+4
Other family	107	22	−5
Professional	51	10	+4
Friend (peer)	153	26	−1
Friend (adult)	22	5	+2
Unspecified	8	2	−2
Other	0	0	−3
Don't know/blank	32	6	−5

(continued)

Table 4–12 (continued)

Vignettes	Mean	Standard Deviation	Mean Change
10. If a friend told me that her stepfather had felt her breasts, I would:			
Tell her to say NO	20	8	+3
Tell professional/cops	27	11	+1
Tell parent/guardian	66	27	+4
Tell someone/get help	85	35	+9
Protect self/defense	5	2	+1
Violent response	10	4	+1
Passive response	2	1	−1
Keep telling until helped	14	6	+5
Don't give advice/take responsibility	3	1	−9
Other	3	1	−11
Don't know/blank	8	3	−5
11. Your sister's boyfriend is pressuring her to have sex. She likes him but is not ready to have sex. What are two things you would tell her to do?			
Say NO/talk	291	60	+17
Tell someone	42	9	+4
Break up	128	24	+15
Violent response	10	2	−3
Passive response	1	1	−4
Other	5	1	−14
Don't know/blank	20	4	−18
12. In the past, John has hit his girlfriend when he was angry. Name two things he could do to stop hurting her when he gets angry again.			
Talk to her	56	12	+2
Alternative expression of anger, destructive	27	6	0
Alternative expression of anger, nondestructive	85	17	+8
Self-awareness (control)	112	13	−3
Time out	68	14	−4
Get help	103	22	+9
Other	1	1	−10
Don't know/blank	36	7	−8

Table 4–12 (continued)

Vignettes	N	Percent	Percent Change
13. Bob has been baby-sitting a one-year-old girl for about four months. Over that time, she has not gained any weight, and looks very quiet and tired most of the time. What should Bob do?			
Talk to baby's parent	122	50	+7
Doctor	53	22	+1
Professional	9	4	+1
Talk with his family/friend	41	17	+10
Avoid/deny	7	3	−1
Other	8	3	−11
Don't know/blank	3	1	−8

	Mean	Standard Deviation	Mean Change
14. If a girl's parents always tell her that she's no good and don't ever let her talk with friends, they are emotionally abusing her.	3.5	.67	+.2
15. If a guy wants sex, he has to pressure a girl.	1.6	.67	−.1
16. If a boy is sexually abused by a man, the boy will probably become gay (homosexual).	1.8	.69	−.2
17. It's hard for girls to say what they really feel about having sex.	2.4	.82	−.2
18. It's difficult for boys to be sensitive and caring with girls when they're expected to be tough and in charge.	2.1	.84	−.2
19. It's fine for a girl to say what she wants, but the guy should have the final say.	1.5	.72	−.2
20. If a teenager was abused as a child, there is no point in reporting because it was too long ago.	1.6	.67	−.1
21. This last year, a father hit his son three times with a belt. Each time he left marks on his son. This is abuse.	3.3	.81	+.2
22. A forty-year-old aunt decides she wants to have sex with her sixteen-year-old nephew. She touches him in a way that turns him on, and then she has sex with him. This is abuse.	3.0	.87	+.1

(*continued*)

Table 4–12 (continued)

Vignettes	Mean	Standard Deviation	Mean Change
23. Mary often has to miss school because her parents make her take care of her brothers and sisters. This is abuse.	2.9	.75	0
24. One night after a party, a boy punches his girlfriend. He apologizes and says it won't happen again. This is abuse.	3.2	.71	+.2
25. A teenager is baby-sitting a three-year-old girl. He gets turned on when he helps her change into her pajamas. This is abuse.	2.3	.69	−.1
26. The same boy (in the last question) puts his hand down the girl's pajama bottoms. This is abuse.	3.5	.62	+.1
27. A fifteen-year-old girl is supposed to be home by 12:00 A.M., but doesn't get home until 3:00 A.M. The next morning her parents tell her to pack some things and not come home until she can live by their rules. This is a case of neglect.	3.0	.80	+1.0

28. Where can this girl go if she doesn't have friends or relatives to turn to?

	N	Percent	Percent Change
Police	16	7	−4
CPS	15	6	+3
Professional/hotline	52	21	+3
School	10	4	−2
Family	5	2	−1
Friend	7	3	+1
Shelter/foster home	92	38	+3
Other (streets)	13	5	−2
Don't know/blank	34	14	−8

Vignettes	Mean	Standard Deviation	Mean Change
29. A teenager is more likely to be abused by a stranger than someone they know.	1.9	.71	−.1

30. Bill got together with Lisa at a party. Lisa enjoyed kissing him, but got nervous when he started touching her below the waist. She started to pull away, but Bill thought she was just being a tease and continued. Lisa became frightened and started to struggle.

Table 4–12 (continued)

Vignettes	N	Percent	Percent Change
Bill seemed so much stronger. She couldn't stop him from having sex with her. This is a cause of rape.	3.3	.77	+ .1
31. Lisa was partly to blame because she led him on.	2.2	.82	+ .2
32. Lisa must have liked it because she didn't make him stop.	1.7	.69	− .3
33. Jack's father always tells him that he will never amount to anything because he's lazy and stupid. This is emotional abuse even though his father is sometimes very nice to him.	3.1	.74	+ .1
34. John had an accident and wrecked his father's car. When his father found out, he lost his temper and beat up John. This is child abuse even though John thought he deserved it.	3.3	.84	+ .3

*The most desired responses are underlined; on multiple choice items, percentages may not sum to 100 because of rounding error and change scores may not sum to zero because of rounding error. On multiple response items, change scores may not sum to zero because the number of responses from pretest to posttest varies.

(see table 4–15). As can be seen, in all cases the scale scores increase from pretest to posttest, and continue to increase from posttest to follow-up.

Similar percentage scale scores for all students (combined) can also be compared at various observations (see table 4–16). Only the combined figures for pretest and follow-up are computed, because the posttest results of the program and control groups cannot be considered equivalent in this design. Again, all scales showed increases from pretest to follow-up.

Overall results of the ANOVA showed significant differences in student scores with group status, student sex, student ethnicity, and to a lesser extent, mother's education. In all subscale scores, girls scored higher than boys. Girls scored significantly higher than boys in the community resources, self-identification, acquaintance rape, emotional abuse, sexual abuse, passive/

Table 4–13
Differences of Scale Scores between Posttest and Follow-up for Program Group

	n	Posttest Mean	Follow-up Mean	t
Date rape	128	15.95	16.45	−2.85**
Emotional abuse	126	21.97	22.66	−3.48***
Physical abuse	125	18.97	19.51	−2.26*
Sexual abuse	126	13.81	14.06	−0.85
Assertiveness	127	16.47	16.73	−1.77
Community resources	132	12.09	12.05	0.13
Neglect	129	8.46	8.70	−1.12
Self-Identification	128	14.36	14.80	−2.04*
Skill Intentions	127	28.98	29.95	−2.27*
Attitude	119	52.22	53.66	−3.34***
Knowledge	127	17.84	17.66	0.67
All	113	99.15	101.64	−3.35***

*p < .05
**p < .01
***p < .001

assertive/aggressive, and overall scales. Significant differences were also found between ethnic groupings in the community resources, physical abuse, emotional abuse, and overall scales; generally, Asian students had lower scores in these scales. When students had mothers with at least a high school education, they scored significantly higher in the community resources and neglect scales, and higher, but not significantly so, in the other scales. Prior class experience made no significant difference on any scale.

Relationships between student and program characteristics and retention of gains in scores were estimated using ANOVA. Gain on the summary score from posttest to follow-up were not correlated with any variable. Pretest to follow-up gains were significant related to mother's education ($r = -.14$; $p < .05$).

Table 4–14

Differences between Mean Program Group Scores at Pretest, Posttest, and Follow-up[1]

	Pretest Mean	Posttest Mean	Follow-up Mean	t(1–2)	t(2–3)	t(1–3)
Date rape	15.09	15.95	16.45	1.84	2.85	3.80***
Emotional abuse	20.89	21.97	22.66	3.51***	3.48***	4.92***
Physical abuse	18.33	18.33	19.51	0.00	2.26*	3.89***
Sexual abuse	12.77	13.81	14.06	1.39	0.85	6.30***
Assertiveness	15.28	16.47	16.73	2.23*	1.77	5.00***
Community resources	10.03	11.26	12.05	3.79***	0.13	6.74***
Neglect	7.50	8.46	8.70	2.58*	1.12	3.45***
Self-Identification	13.50	14.36	14.80	2.26*	2.04*	4.33***
Skill intentions	25.81	28.98	29.95	3.73***	2.27*	8.45***
Attitude	49.53	52.22	53.66	3.24**	3.34***	6.38***
Knowledge	15.85	17.84	17.66	4.73***	0.67	5.04***
All	91.43	99.15	101.64	5.78***	3.35***	9.35***

*p < .05
**p < .01
***p < .001
[1]n varies from 105 to 132 because of missing cases

Class Evaluation Survey

The class evaluation survey was given to students in the program group at the time of the first posttest. The survey is designed to measure the "consumer response" of high school students in the program group to the CAPTA programs. In general, the results show overwhelmingly positive evaluations of how well CAPTA programs met their goals: 89 percent of the students felt they learned a lot from the class, and 92 percent felt the information would help them prevent child abuse or assault (see table 4–17). Almost 67 percent of the students felt they were now less likely to be abused. Although adolescents would be expected to mistrust adults, particularly with regard to such a sensitive issue as

Table 4–15
Percentage of Possible Program Group Scores at Pretest, Posttest, and Follow-up

	Pretest (n = 247)	Posttest	Follow-up (n = 247)	1–2	2–3 (n = 133)	1–3
Date rape	77.3	78.6	81.8	1.3	3.2	4.5
Emotional abuse	78.5	80.9	83.6	2.4	2.7	5.1
Physical abuse	77.2	78.0	80.9	0.8	2.9	3.7
Sexual abuse	71.6	74.7	77.7	3.1	3.0	6.1
Assertiveness	86.9	89.9	92.6	3.0	2.7	5.7
Community resources	50.8	58.5	60.2	7.7	1.7	9.4
Neglect	64.1	68.9	72.1	4.8	3.2	8.0
Self-Identification	76.2	78.5	82.2	2.3	3.7	6.0
Skill intentions	71.1	76.3	80.9	5.2	4.6	9.8
Attitude	73.9	75.9	78.4	2.0	2.5	4.5
Knowledge	66.9	73.0	74.1	6.1	1.1	7.2
Summary	72.0	75.6	79.0	3.6	3.4	7.0

Table 4–16
Percentage of Correct Scores Each Scale for Program and Control Groups Combined

Scale Correct	Pretest Change	Percent Mean	Follow-up Correct	Percent Mean	Percent
Date rape	15.4	76.9	16.3	81.6	4.5
Emotional abuse	21.3	78.8	22.4	83.1	4.3
Physical abuse	18.6	77.7	19.5	81.1	3.4
Sexual abuse	13.4	74.2	13.7	75.9	1.7
Assertiveness	15.7	87.0	16.1	89.6	2.6
Community resources	13.6	68.0	14.0	70.0	2.0
Neglect	09.2	76.9	09.5	79.3	2.4
Self-Identification	14.2	78.8	14.8	82.2	3.4
Skill intentions	26.5	71.6	29.6	79.9	8.3
Attitude	50.3	74.0	53.3	78.4	4.4
Knowledge	15.9	66.2	17.1	74.2	8.0
Summary*	99.1	76.8	102.8	79.7	2.9

*Sum of means does not equal the summary score because scales had overlapping items.

Table 4–17
Class Evaluation Survey

	Mean*	SD
I learned a lot from the class.	3.0	0.6
The class was boring.	2.0	0.6
We had time to ask questions and discuss.	3.0	0.7
We were told when and where we could talk alone with the speaker or other adults.	3.2	0.6
I felt comfortable with the things we talked about.	3.0	0.6
This information will help me.	3.2	0.6
I could understand the information.	3.3	0.5
The class will make teenagers worry more than they need to.	2.0	0.6
I am now less likely to be abused.	2.7	0.8
I am now more likely to tell an adult I trust if I or someone I know is abused.	3.1	0.6
If I were abused, I still would not report it.	1.7	0.6
In what grade should this class first be given?		
8th 169 9th 53 10th 10 11th 4 12th 2 (71.0%) (22.3%) (4.2%) (1.7%) (.8%)		
I wish I had this information before now to protect myself from child abuse or assault.	2.8	0.7
I found the information from the program helpful in preventing child abuse or assault.	3.2	0.6
The information from the program helped me recognize someone who I think was abused or assaulted.	2.5	0.8

*(1) Strongly Disagree; (2) Disagree; (3) Agree; (4) Strongly Agree.

child abuse, 93 percent of the students reported that they were now more likely to tell a trusted adult about child abuse. About half of the students indicated that they had already used the information to recognize someone who had been abused. Finally, 94 percent told us that the presenters announced when and where they could talk alone with a professional.

Those students who indicated that they still would not report whether they were abused (about 7 percent of the total) gave a variety of reasons. The most common reason given was that the student would still feel too embarrassed. One student indicated that he "would feel gay." Some of the students showed a lingering mistrust of adults, stating that reporting probably would not help or that relatives would not believe them. Concern about the attitudes of peers surfaced as well; for example, one student felt that others would look at her as if she were strange and confused. Cultural norms also were apparent; one Asian student stated that "it is against our religion to turn against your parents."

One issue that has generated considerable interest is whether child abuse prevention programs unnecessarily create negative effects in students. The negative effects are fairly minimal; 89 percent of the students reported that they felt comfortable with the things that were discussed in the class while 16 percent thought that the classes make teenagers worry more than necessary.

Students generally seemed to approve of the teaching methods used in the programs; 86 percent of the students did not find the class boring, and 86 percent felt they had time to ask questions and discuss. Programs apparently were sensitive to the developmental level of students as well; 99 percent reported that they could understand the information provided.

The survey gives PPP administrators some indications of what teaching methods work best. About one-third of the students liked the discussion the best, about one-fourth preferred the presentation by the speaker, about 18 percent chose role-plays, and 10 percent liked video/films. Only 4 percent liked asking questions the best. Not all programs employed all of these techniques, so these percentages are difficult to interpret.

Interesting feedback was generated about the timing of adolescent level CAPTA programs. Approximately 71 percent of students recommended that the curricula should be given before the high school years. Over two-thirds of the students also wished that they had the information from the programs earlier in their lives.

Relationships between class evaluation scores and categorical demographic variables were estimated using ANOVA. Girls tended to rate the programs higher ($p<.06$ level) than boys. No significant differences in rating were found regarding student ethnicity, mothers' level of education, family composition, and prior experience with child abuse classes.

Student Interviews

Students were asked a series of fifteen open-ended questions in an interview format. Everyone of the seventy-two students interviewed had a generally positive overall response to the CAPTA program they were given. About nine out of ten students felt child abuse is a problem for teens. Most of the students had at least some prior knowledge of child abuse, but only 23 percent stated that they had talked with their parents about the subject. Usually if they had talked with their parents, the discussion was about stranger danger and how to say no and go tell.

Strikingly, 87 percent of the students indicated that they would still have difficulty telling an adult that they were abused, preferring instead to tell a close peer. Of those who said they would tell someone, 35 percent preferred to tell a close friend, 34 percent a family member, and 25 percent a professional in the school or community. Although almost nine out of ten remembered that they were told they could speak with someone after the CAPTA program, only 30 percent said they would have felt comfortable doing so. A few who said they would report qualified their response by saying that they would only report if the abuse was "serious." Many stated that they would feel embarrassed or would fear retaliation.

A variety of other responses were elicited. Although one-quarter of the students reported no change in their thoughts about dating, another quarter (all girls) reported that they were now more careful about who they dated. About 8 percent (all boys) stated that they are now more considerate of their partners, and 3 percent (all boys) said that they are more careful because they now know that they can go to jail for date rape. Over one-half of the students stated that the programs made them think about themselves as future parents (even though none of the programs had specified that making students more sensitive to parenting issues was a goal).

When asked what is the best way to prevent child abuse, 27 percent suggested public education, 20 percent asked to have parents be taught alternatives to abuse, and 9 percent recommended more punishment for offenders or protective removal of the child. The remaining had no specific suggestions. Only 49 percent could indicate what the most important thing was that they learned: self-identification as a possible abuser (17 percent), self-protection (fourteen percent), avoiding date rape (fourteen percent), and emotional abuse (4 percent).

The adolescents had some recommendations for child abuse prevention instructors. They would improve the program by having teen victims speak (38 percent), by using peer teachers (6 percent), and by explaining the effects that child abuse has on victims (6 percent). About 4 percent suggested each of the following improvements: have more time, use small groups, and let students talk more. Every student but one preferred that CAPTA classes be taught in small classes rather than in a large assembly. When asked whether child abuse by adults or acquaintance rape was more important, 27 percent preferred child abuse by adults 19 percent wanted acquaintance rape, and 54 percent asked for both to be taught.

Parent Interviews

Interviewed parents $(n=23)$ almost uniformly stated that child abuse is a problem for adolescents and their families. Of the various forms of child maltreatment, parents were the least likely to call acquaintance rape and abduction forms of child abuse. However, fully 100 percent believed that the subject of date rape should be taught to adolescents in the schools. Although 96 percent of the parents knew about child abuse reporting laws, 22 percent thought (incorrectly) that parents were required by law to report. About 87 percent thought child abuse prevention should be taught to teens in the schools, but about one in six cautioned that schools should not "go to extremes." Although not asked, 39 percent added that child abuse prevention should be started earlier than high school.

Although 96 percent of the parents said that they had talked with their children about child abuse, only 13 percent stated that this had occurred only after the CAPTA class. None of the parents felt that the CAPTA program had made their child unnecessarily worried. Parents had about the same level of concern that their child would be a victim of child abuse and victim of acquaintance rape, and a little less concerned about their child someday abusing someone else.

Parents had concerns about the coordination of classroom program efforts with parents. Many (78 percent) of the parents reported that the schools did not inform them enough about the CAPTA program their child took. About the same number (74 percent) also reported that they did not know that a parent's program was offered.

When asked what is the best way to stop child abuse, the parents suggested teaching parents skills and/or attitudes (35 percent), early education of children (30 percent), stricter punishment of offenders (17 percent), teaching both parents and children (13 percent), and religion (13 percent). When asked what should be changed about the program, some parents wanted better teachers (9 percent) and more parenting education (9 percent); most (82 percent) did not know.

PPP Staff Interviews

Staff interviews with ten child abuse prevention staff (including seven program directors) found that respondents have worked with child maltreatment programs for an average of 5.2 years. Prior to their prevention work, three were teachers, two were social workers, one was a probation officer, and one was a drug abuse prevention specialist. Only three had previous work experience with adolescents. When asked what qualities a good, adolescent-level CAPTA teacher should have, the respondents gave a variety of responses, including genuineness, honesty, openness, ability to relate, sensitivity, commitment to self-growth, high energy, and a fondness for adolescents.

Although half of the PPP staff felt that student response was generally positive, half also felt that boys were more resistant to acquaintance rape curricula than girls. In fact, half of the staff also commented that girls are generally more attentive to PPP programs and more willing to disclose. Some (20 percent) commented that Hispanic students were as a group more resistant to acquaintance rape curricula, and that minority students tend to see adolescent abuse as just one of many problems they must face.

When asked about which parts of the curricula worked best, the respondents gave a number of impressions. They believe that students like role-plays (40 percent), film and video (40 percent), speakers who are victims of abuse (30 percent), and discussion (30 percent). Also mentioned were self-defense (20 percent) and an exciting presenter (20 percent).

Only 30 percent stated that they had contact with students' parents. However, no staff member reported ever taking a complaint about the program from a parent. When asked why parents do not come to parent group meetings, they suggested that parents are tired (20 percent), parents have lost interest as their children grew older (20 percent), and parents were working (10 percent).

None of the staff members felt that the child abuse prevention programs make students unnecessarily suspicious of other people. Instead, they suggested that the information they teach empowers students (20 percent), that they teach awareness instead of fear (20 percent), and the problem is so severe that it is actually difficult to frighten students too much (30 percent). About a third of the staff felt that students have significant misconceptions about child maltreatment; including the idea that victims are responsible, the idea that child abuse happens to younger children rather than to adolescents, confusion about definitions of abuse, and false ideas about sexuality.

About 30 percent of the staff hoped that, in the long term, child abuse prevention programs will change the values and attitudes of adolescents, and about 20 percent hoped that some forms of adolescent maltreatment will be reduced. Almost two-thirds asked for more funding so that topics can be covered adequately.

Almost-one third of the staff thought that better cooperation and coordination with high schools is desirable. Less indication was given that coordination with community organizations located outside of the school was equally desirable, although one program did include a police officer as a speaker in the program.

All of the staff felt that the program would be most effective when given in small groups rather than in assembly-size meetings. About half of the staff suggested that they simply did not have the resources to also work with special education youth, and recommended that special education teachers take over that responsibility themselves.

High School Staff Interviews

High school staff ($n = 8$) included three administrators, two teachers, one nurse, and two school counselors. Only one-fourth were family life teachers. These respondents had worked in high schools for an average length of 13.5 years. About two-thirds had an overall positive impression of high school–level programs, and all the staff felt that such programs belong in the high schools. Only two of the staff had taught adolescent maltreatment prevention content to a high school class.

None of the respondents had ever attended workshops provided by a PPP. None of the respondents reported being aware of any follow-up provided by CAPTA staff after the programs. Three-fourths of the high school staff thought that high school staff could not currently do as good a job as PPP staff did in teaching the CAPTA programs. Little indication was given about whether they thought that high school staff could improve their teaching of prevention programs with additional training. Several staff suggested that at least some teachers already feel overwhelmed and overworked and have little enthusiasm for being asked to teach new curricula.

Staff who were not family life teachers were no more likely than family life education teachers to report that they could do as good a job as CAPTA staff. School counselors were more likely than other school staff to report that high school staff could do as good a job as CAPTA staff.

Although 38 percent reported that school administrators and the community supported child abuse prevention programs, 38 percent also reported the opposite. None of the staff wanted to see child abuse prevention programs taught in assembly-size groups, preferring small, classroom-size groups. When asked if acquaintance rape or child abuse by adults was more important, 75 percent felt that they deserve equal priority, 13 percent choose acquaintance rape, and 13 percent choose child abuse by adults.

In an effort to further this discussion, two self-defense experts were interviewed, both independent from the high schools and CAPTA programs. These experts, who had previous experience working with adolescents, were asked what they thought about the effectiveness of brief self-defense trainings, such as those done in some of the child abuse prevention programs. Both men suggested that, as a group, adolescents have a particularly wide range of physical and psychological maturity, and that the instructor would not have any control over whether students might at a later time use the skills taught in either a destructive or constructive manner. They suggested that students would need at minimum a dozen contact hours of class time to be adequately taught self-defense skills. However, both respondents believe that, overall, it is better to give students a little self-defense training than none at all.

Law Enforcement Interviews

Law enforcement staff $(n = 8)$ were all officers who were working with child and adolescent maltreatment cases. These officers had worked an average of fourteen years in law enforcement. When asked their overall impressions of the programs, the officers reported that the good touch/bad touch section was too ambiguous (38 percent), that they often have received inappropriate referrals from child abuse prevention staff (38 percent), and that the program was a good one (13 percent). A full 25 percent reported having had cases involving adolescents who had a child abuse prevention program. They did not report whether the programs occurred before or after cases were opened.

The legislatively described components of CAPTA programs were described to the officers. In general, the majority tended to think that these components were important and achievable goals. When asked how well the programs taught students to disclose, 38 percent stated that the programs did a good job, while 25 percent said the programs did a better job with younger children. Regarding how well safety and self-disclosure was taught, two-thirds were unsure, and again reference was made to a better job being done with younger children. One fourth suggested that a good job was done teaching students about their right to live free from abuse; one-fourth felt a poor job was being done, and one officer felt that a better job was done with younger children. Two-thirds of the officers thought that the programs did not do a good job providing crises counseling and reporting for students.

Again, concerns were raised about the coordination between the classroom prevention efforts and other prevention efforts in the school and community at large. Two-thirds of those interviewed felt that a poor job was done teaching parents and high school teachers. Two-thirds also stated that they themselves had not been adequately informed about child abuse prevention high school programs.

All of the officers wanted child abuse prevention staff to better understand the functions and limits of law enforcement. All of the officers thought that law enforcement should be more involved in child abuse prevention programs, but half of the officers said they are personally too busy to become more involved. When asked what should be changed about adolescent-level child abuse prevention programs, the officers asked for appropriate interviewing during disclosures (38 percent), more confidentiality in interviewing (25 percent), longer programs (38 percent), and cross-training with CAPTA and law enforcement staffs (25 percent). In addition, they called for more information to be taught to students regarding how law enforcement works (25 percent) and less emphasis paid to self-defense.

Child Protective Service Interviews

Interviews with child protective service (CPS) social workers ($n = 7$) were conducted with experienced people who have worked in child protective services for an average of 10.3 years. CPS workers were nominated by the programs as knowledgeable about CAPTA. About 60 percent thought that they had been adequately informed about high school–level child abuse prevention programs. When asked for overall impressions, the social workers often commented about the referrals they received. They suggested that most referrals were too vague at first, and that they had subsequently become more appropriate (43 percent). Only one had ever had a case involving an adolescent who was known to have taken a child abuse prevention program and had subsequently reported her abuse.

The mandated components of CAPTA programs were also described to the social workers. In general, the majority tended to think that these components were important and achievable goals. When asked how well the programs taught students to disclose, 43 percent stated that the programs did a good job, while 29 percent were not sure. Some of the social workers (29 percent) stated the programs did a good job teaching students how and where to get help. Regarding how well safety and self-disclosure was taught, 43 percent suggested that the programs did not do a very good job. One-fourth stated that the programs did a good job teaching self-defense techniques, and 71 percent felt a good job was done teaching students about their right to live free from abuse. About 43 percent of the social workers stated that the programs did a good job providing crisis counseling and reporting for students, and 14 percent also thought that a poor job was done teaching parents and high school teachers.

The CPS workers, like the law enforcement officers, wanted to see greater coordination of prevention efforts on a community-wide basis. Almost half of the social workers wanted PPP staff to be more aware of the limitations of the CPS system, and to improve their ability to make appropriate referrals. All of the social workers thought that they should be more involved in CAPTA programs.

Definitional Survey

As explained above, the responses of students, their parents, and various professionals to eleven definitional items from the pretest questionnaire were collected. ANOVA was not used because of large differences in group size. Instead, *t*-tests were used to assess differences between the means (see appendix E). Overall, students at pretest tended to score lowest of the three groups; they tended to be least likely to evaluate certain situations as being abusive. Parents tended to score in the middle ranges. Professionals tended to score the highest as a group; they were the most likely to evaluate the situations as being abusive.

Significant (.05 level) differences were found using *t*-tests between the various groups on items in the definitional scale. As indicated below, high scores on these items indicate desired responses. Therefore, if group A scores higher than group B, this suggests that group A tends to define child abuse more adequately than group B. Professionals and parents both scored significantly higher than students on items measuring responses to all the forms of maltreatment, including those involving neglect, psychological maltreatment, physical abuse, date rape, and sexual abuse. Although professionals scored higher than parents on all but two items, parents did score significantly (.05 level) higher than professionals on an item on psychological maltreatment (item 33) and higher, but not significantly, on an item on sexual abuse (item 22). Professionals scored significantly (.05 level) higher than parents on items regarding neglect (item 23), sexual abuse (item 26), and physical abuse (item 34). There was no clear pattern from the data that indicated significant differences between the major forms of child maltreatment (sexual abuse, physical abuse, psychological maltreatment, and neglect), in terms of how the three groups evaluated them.

Peer-Taught and Adult-Taught Prevention

A comparison of a peer-taught group, adult-taught group, and control (using the same delayed, cross-over method of control) group was completed at the San Francisco PPP site. Using ANOVA techniques, differences between the scale scores of students who were peer-taught ($n = 34$), adult-taught ($n = 20$), or in the control group ($n = 35$) were tested for each observation. On pretest scores, no significant differences were found among any of the three groups on any scale.

Analysis of variance (ANOVA) with gain scores from pretest to posttest (shown in table 4–18), showed that the peer-taught group did in fact have a significantly (.05) higher gain score on the summary scale, as compared to the adult-taught and control groups. The only other scale that showed significant (.05 level) differences in pretest to posttest gain scores was emotional abuse. No significant differences were found in gain scores from pretest to follow-up or posttest to follow-up.

Comparisons of posttest and follow-up scale scores on community resources showed a significant drop for the peer-taught and adult-taught students in the program group. All scores went up significantly for the adult-taught and control groups. No sig-

Table 4–18

Comparison of Peer-Taught, Adult-Taught, and Control Groups Gain Scores from Pretest to Posttest

Scale	Peer-Taught ($n = 34$)	Adult-Taught ($n = 20$)	Control ($n = 35$)	F
Date rape	-0.07	0.29	-0.02	.41
Emotional abuse	1.41	-0.29	-0.22	5.39*
Physical abuse	0.34	-0.65	-0.11	1.03
Sexual abuse	0.66	0.18	0.02	1.11
Assertiveness	0.93	0.53	0.16	2.03
Community resources	1.00	1.00	0.56	0.32
Neglect	0.14	-0.07	0.93	1.40
Self-Identification	0.79	0.60	0.19	0.49
Skill intentions	1.62	1.87	0.67	1.00
Attitude	1.76	0.20	0.47	1.28
Knowledge	1.66	1.47	0.16	2.61
Summary	5.03	3.53	1.30	3.21*

*$p < .05$

Table 4–19

Percentage of Total Possible Score of Each Group for Summary Scale at Pretest, Posttest, and Follow-up

Group	Pretest	Posttest	Follow-up
Peer-Taught	69.1	72.6	74.5
Adult-Taught	71.6	74.0	76.1
Control	68.9	69.1	75.3

nificant differences between peer-taught and adult-taught students were found in how they scored on the class evaluation survey. Only the nature of the instructor had a significant (.05 level) relationship with overall initial gain scale scores. No independent variable was found to have a significant effect on retention gain scale scores (from posttest to follow-up). An analysis of the changes in percentage of total possible scores appears in table 4–19.

Comparisons of Relative Strengths of Factors For Total Group

Pretest

In preparation to construct a regression model, Pearson's correlations were run on the total scores of all three observations. Pretest correlations showed that the summary scale except for age and group had significant (.05 level) relationships with gender (higher for girls, $r=.35$; $p<.001$): class (higher for more previous education, $r=.08$; $p<.052$): mother's education (higher for more education, $r=.20$; $p<.001$): ethnicity (higher for whites, $r=.23$; $p<.001$): and number of parents at home (higher for one parent; $r=.12$, $p<.01$). Posttest results were similar, except that program group membership was also significantly correlated with the total score. Follow-up results showed fewer patterns; student gender had the strongest correlations with the scales; again, girls scored significantly ($r=.19$; $p<.001$) higher. Analysis of the student evaluation items showed a significant negative correlation ($r = -.10$; p<.05) between mother's education and the total score; students whose mothers had less education tended to rate the program higher.

Multiple regression analysis using the summary pretest scores showed four significant (.01 level) independent variables (see table 4–20). These were, in order beginning with the most powerful: sex, mother's education, ethnicity, and living with two parents. The R^2 value was .25. A regression run with student evaluation total scores found only mother's education as a significant (.05 level) demographic predictor. The R^2 value was only .02.

Gain Scores

Correlations were also calculated with gain scores to see what factors were related to learning. Only one significant relationship was found between an independent demographic variable and a scale gain score: students who lived with two parents tended to have higher overall initial gain scores. The "live-with" variable had a strong negative correlation with mother's education. The variables chosen for inclusion in the regression analysis were therefore selected because they seemed to have reasonable correlations with the scale observation and gain scores and because

Table 4–20
Regression Analysis of Summary Scores at Pretest

Significant	B	SE of B	F
Sex	8.13	.93	
Mother's education	4.55	1.03	−4.40*
Ethnicity	3.34	1.01	3.31*
Live with mother	−2.42	.97	−2.50*
Class	1.19	1.12	1.06
Time	0.61	0.73	.83
Age	−.19	.39	−.49
Group	.77	.93	.83
R^2 = .25			

*p < .01

they were not strongly correlated with each other. The variables included in the regression analyses were sex, mother's education, ethnicity, age, previous classes, and group.

Multiple regression was also performed with gain scores (see table 4–21). Items were entered as they explained variance, with

Table 4–21
Regression Analyses of Summary Gain Score

Variables	B	Se of B	T
Pretest to Posttest, Program Group (R^2 = .06)			
Live with two parents	2.72	1.03	2.63*
Ethnicity	−1.73	1.21	−1.43
Time	1.06	0.80	1.32
Class	0.70	1.31	0.54
Sex	0.64	1.10	0.58
Mother's education	−0.56	1.18	−0.48
Age	0.09	0.38	0.23
Posttest to Follow-up, Program Group (R^2 = .05)			
Sex	−1.70	1.62	−1.05
Time	−1.63	1.25	−1.31
Live with two parents	1.47	1.78	0.83
Class	−1.43	1.91	−0.75
Mother's education	−0.75	1.76	−0.43
Ethnicity	−0.70	1.77	−0.39
Age	0.28	0.44	0.62
Pretest to Follow-up, Both Groups (R^2 = .04)			
Mother's education	−2.12	1.21	−1.75
Class	−1.47	1.26	−1.16
Time	−1.12	0.91	−0.13
Ethnicity	−1.12	1.11	−0.11
Age	0.67	0.37	1.82
Live with two parents	0.57	1.22	0.47
Sex	0.53	1.04	0.50
Group	0.26	1.03	0.25

*p < .01

the exception of group and time, which were entered last. Regression for total scale gain scores from pretest to posttest showed that only the variable that described students who lived with two parents was a significant predictor: students with two parents tended to learn more than those with one parent. Regression for total scale gain scores from posttest to follow-up showed no significant predictors. Regression for total gain scores from pretest to follow-up also had no significant predictors.

Family Life Programs

The survey of adolescent maltreatment prevention programs in California and other states revealed that family life programs in high schools often teach some of the curricula covered in high school level CAPTA programs. Professionals ($n = 8$) in selected states were contacted. Five states (Michigan, Iowa, Virginia, Wisconsin, and Massachusetts) were found to be currently developing comprehensive guidelines for family life or health education that integrate some child maltreatment issues from kindergarten through high school. A variety of approaches are used in teaching child maltreatment prevention in these states. Some schools use specially trained health or family life educators, while other schools ask regular teachers to cover the material. There also appears to be a trend in these states of keeping parallel systems of visitor-and teacher-delivered programs intact. There is some indication of a movement toward having outside experts train high school teachers to deliver child abuse content.

State-by-State Survey

Key results of the state-by-state Survey are shown in table 4–22. Funding and coordination of adolescent maltreatment prevention programs were found to be variable across the sixteen states studies. In some states, no state funding is made available for such programs; when funding is available it may be administered by the department of public instruction, the children's trust fund, or by an office of prevention.

Table 4-22
State Survey of High School Child Maltreatment Prevention at a Glance

State	Coordination and Funding	Mandate	Emphasis Relative to Other Ages	Relative Emphasis of Curricula Type*	Relative Emphasis of Forms of Maltreatment	Notes
Illinois	Dept. of Children and Family Services $250,000, 1 year	Yes	Preschool and Elementary	Preparenting Acquaintance Rape	Sexual All others	Recommends training teachers
Washington	Superintendent of Public Instruction $225,000, 2 years	Yes	Elementary Preschool Middle High School	Preparenting Abuse by Adults Acquaintance Rape	Sexual Physical Neglect Psychological	Teen pregnancy Perinatal program
New Mexico	Human Services $177,515, 18 mos.	No	Elementary Middle High School	No	Sexual Physical and Neglect Psychological	Innovative outward bound training of peers
Oregon	No state plan Trust fund $285,000, 1 year	No	Middle and High School	Preparenting Abuse by Adults Acquaintance Rape	Physical Neglect All others	Perinatal programs Need more research
Delaware	Office of Prevention	No	No	Sex Offender Prevention Preparenting	Sexual Physical Neglect Psychological	Start Acquaintance Rape in Middle School; self-identification of offenders

(continued)

Table 4–22 (continued)

State	Coordination and Funding	Mandate	Emphasis Relative to Other Ages	Relative Emphasis of Curricula Type*	Relative Emphasis of Forms of Maltreatment	Notes
Michigan	Children's Trust Fund $250,000, 1 year	No	Elementary and Middle	No	Sexual (99 percent)	Mostly theatrical programs
Oklahoma	OCAP in Health Department $212,000, 1 year	No	Elementary K–4	Personal Safety Preparenting	Sexual	35 projects Assertiveness skills
New York	DSS	No	No	Acquaintance Rape Preparenting Abuse of Adults	No	Theatre groups
Kansas	DSS Children's Trust Fund $166,000, 1 year	No	Elementary Preschool Middle High School	No	No	Interest in High School growing I'm in charge Step teen
Minnesota	Dept. of Human Services	No	No	Sexual Abuse Preparenting	Sexual Abuse	Sharp - offender prevention Illusion theater Climb theater
Iowa	Dept. of Public Instruction $50,000, 1 year	Yes (Family Life)	No	Sexual Abuse	Sexual Physical All Others	High School emphasis increasing choices and changes, Adolescent Sex Abuse

State	Coordination and Funding	Mandate	Emphasis Relative to Other Ages	Relative Emphasis of Curricula Type*	Relative Emphasis of Forms of Maltreatment	Notes
Wisconsin	Children's Trust Fund $100,000, 4 years	No	Elementary Teen Parents	No	No	Theatrical groups Illusion theater
Florida	Dept. of Education (Teen parents)	No	No	Parenting Preparenting	No	Teen parent program
Virginia	CPS/NCPCA $400,000	No	No	Parenting Sexuality	No	Family Life, New program next year K–12
Texas	Children's Trust Fund	No	No	Abuse by Adults Acquaintance Rape	No	Red Cross Presentations
Ohio	Children's Trust Fund $100,000	No	Elementary Preschool All others	Preparenting Abuse by Adults Acquaintance Rape	No	School-based program Family Life

*In order from highest priority (top) to lowest (bottom).

California's CAPTA program is by far the best-funded state program; no state was found to spend even 5 percent of the yearly CAPTA budget. The budgets shown in table 4–22 can also be considered from the standpoint of per capita spending. Thus, each year, California spends about fifty cents per capita; Oregon eleven cents; New Mexico nine cents; and Kansas, Virginia, and Oklahoma seven cents each. Michigan and Washington spend three cents, Illinois and Iowa two cents, and Ohio and Wisconsin less than one cent per capita each year. Because it is quite possible that each of the states mentioned here actually spend more on adolescent maltreatment than was determined in this survey, these results should be interpreted with caution.

Although a number of states apparently are now seeking to change their laws, only three states surveyed—California, Illinois, and Washington—were found to currently have mandated adolescent maltreatment prevention programs. Of the nine states that apparently prioritize prevention efforts by age, eight emphasize programs for children younger than middle school age; California is similar in this respect as well. Although California's programs generally emphasize prevention of adolescent maltreatment by their peers or by adults, seven out of twelve states reporting indicated that the highest priority is currently given to preparenting or parenting education (in this evaluation, this content is included in the scale called self-identification). However, eight out of nine states reporting indicated that they emphasize sexual abuse more than either physical abuse, psychological maltreatment, or neglect.

5
Redesigning Classroom Child Abuse Prevention

Program Structure, Staff, and Curriculum

Almost all (90 percent) of the child abuse prevention programs were visitor-delivered by staff from community-based child abuse or rape crisis agencies, with the remainder delivered by high school staff. (Although only a few programs are teacher-delivered, these are some of the largest programs.) Each agency must make arrangements to present in each school, as the enabling legislation does not require that schools cooperate with the PPPs. In five of the six service areas studied, PPP staff reported spending considerable amounts of time trying to gain permission to teach students in particular high schools, sometimes having to seek permission from the schools year after year.

Los Angeles Unified Schools is one exception to visitor-delivered child abuse prevention classes. In their model, high school teachers are trained to deliver the CAPTA program. Teachers have responded well to the program and a cadre of trained presenters is emerging as a day-in and day-out resource to youth in Los Angeles. Some of the apparent advantages of the program were witnessed in additional site visits to the Los Angeles Unified School District. First, because all child abuse prevention providers are also school employees, communication links between prevention specialists and the high school staff are enhanced, and the prevention program content tends to be integrated with other school curricula. Similarly, high school teachers seem to be more likely to cooperate with prevention efforts when initiated by school system employees than by outside experts. Second, because prevention programs are taught by experienced teams composed of high school staff members, the teachers of the programs tend to be competent in dealing with adolescents, knowledgeable about group and classroom dynamics, and sensitive to local and school issues. Third, the program director, who is also a school employee, has the benefit of knowledge of and rapport with key school administrators. Only one of the six programs that we studied intensively had a history of association with the L.A. schools. Although we believe in the logic of the approach, the performance of students in this program was not strikingly different from that of other students. According to the program staff, however, at the time of the evaluation, this program was not fully incorporating the school-based model.

High school CAPTA programs generally do not intervene at the family, school, or community level. Whereas 85 percent of the PPPs at least make an effort to have parent meetings, fewer than four parents attended a typical one-time-only meeting. Meetings typically focused on discussion of the content that students would learn in their classes and gave little attention to enhancing parenting skills to reduce parent-adolescent conflict. Nor do high school programs accomplish significant work with other community professionals, including high school staff, law enforcement staff, and CPS workers. Most parents and teachers interviewed stated that they were not invited to any child abuse prevention training. Overall, child abuse prevention staff do not make as much of an effort to reduce the general vulnerability of children through "coordination with and training for parents and school staff" (State of California, Assembly Bill 2443, 18975.7a) as they do through direct presentations to students.

Many in the professional and public community are still unaware of the purpose and nature of CAPTA. Although not mandated, few cross-training programs are set up between child abuse prevention staff, child protective service workers, law enforcement officers, and social service providers or teachers. Almost every professional interviewed did state that they thought more interprofessional cooperation was needed in designing and implementing high school level CAPTA programs.

Staffing

Presenters of child abuse prevention content had varied and often considerable prior experience working in the helping professions as volunteers, teachers, social workers, and probations officers. However, few had much experience working directly with adolescent populations and fewer still had direct knowledge of the literature on adolescent development and teaching methodologies. Although their agencies served a multiracial clientele, the six program executive administrators were white and female, and only one of the six presenters of the training was not white and female.

There was a high turnover rate of staff in delivering child abuse prevention content. During the two years of the evaluation project, key staff members primarily responsible for teaching adolescents in all of the six programs under study left their positions. This is particularly disturbing given the fact that these PPPs are among the best established in the state and might be expected to have lower rates of turnover. Such a turnover rate stretches already thin resources for delivering services to cover additional recruiting and training. More troubling, such turnover all but preempts the programs from articulating and implementing a long-range plan that builds on past experience and refines the program. We would not expect such turnover if the programs were administered by the school districts.

The ecological model indicates that persons exposed to the most social and family stressors are most likely to be victims and victimizers. Given their disproportionate exposure to ecological stress and violence, students from ethnic minorities and various subcultures may require special curricula examples and methodologies. More minority and male teachers and administrators may also be required. PPP administrators and presenters should reflect the diversity of cultural and linguistic backgrounds representative of each local population. Similarly, peer teachers and counselors should also reflect the diversity of the student populations they serve.

Curriculum

High school child abuse prevention curricula in California vary widely and include an average of twenty topics. Most last about two classroom periods (a total of about hundred minutes) and are delivered by staff from community-based prevention programs. Primary prevention programs included at least twenty-seven areas of program content, with the greatest emphasis given to: (1) acquaintance rape, (2) definitions and dynamics of child abuse, (3) assertiveness training, (4) self-empowerment, (5) children's rights, and (6) sexual abuse. Areas receiving the least emphasis were physical abuse by adults and peers, emotional abuse, parenting education, healthy sexuality, homosexuality/homophobia, self-identification as a (potential) perpetrator, sexual harassment, stranger rape, and abduction. Strategies to prevent the abuse of younger children by adolescents are given little consideration.

Little evidence was found that length of class or any teaching method, including the peer-teaching model, was more effective than any other. Although there was some evidence that length of class had more positive effect on retention of knowledge than on initial gains, the effects are small. Student gains scores from the peer-taught method were not significantly higher than those from the adult-taught program.

What Students Learn

Students who received the CAPTA program had statistically significant increases in knowledge, attitudes, and intended skills about emotional abuse, sexual abuse, assertiveness, and community resources from pretest to posttest. Learning about neglect, self-identification as a possible offender, and physical abuse was not demonstrated. Learning about acquaintance rape was not demonstrated, in spite of the relatively large emphasis given to this content area.

Students who received the training had scores at the four-month follow-up that were higher than their posttest scores. By follow-up, all scores were significantly higher than at pretest and more than half the scores were significantly higher than at posttest. No demographic variables were found to have significant effect on gain scores with this group. (Comparisons between the program and control group cannot be made at follow-up because all students had received the CAPTA program by then; thus, changes in follow-up scores that are attributable to influences other than CAPTA cannot be separated from those due to CAPTA.) The knowledge and attitude gains are particularly remarkable, given the large number of topics and brief amount of time that the presenters had with the students. The continued gain after posttest may at least in part reflect a "sensitivity effect," in which students continue to interact with each other (and with other members of their families, schools, and communities) regarding adolescent maltreatment. It may also indicate that students learned child abuse content in subsequent health or family life classes or elsewhere.

Measures of the probability of an event are not the same as measures of the magnitude of an event. The finding of significant positive effect on student scores "leads to a further task which is to describe the effect" (Friedman 1968, p. 250). Although statistically significant gains were found, the effect sizes of the gains were small. Only 23 percent of students who took the class learned more than they would have if they had not taken it, and only one of six students who took CAPTA learned at least 10 percent more than students who did not. The average overall gains were less than 10 percent. Participation in the program explained only 5 percent of knowledge scores at program end. In contrast 61 percent of the summary knowledge score was explained by the students' preprogram knowledge. In other words, the gains, although statistically significant, appear to have modest *substantive* significance.

In interpreting substantive significance, the brief duration of the actual instruction period needs to be considered again. On one hand, the fact that the average program lasted only hundred minutes yet contained twenty (somewhat overlapping) topic areas makes any positive change recorded after four months rather remarkable. On the other hand, the brevity of each topic presentation also suggests that child abuse prevention resources are spread very thin, and that increased student learning may be even more efficiently generated. Ways to increase efficiency will be described in the recommendations section of this chapter and in the final chapter.

Child abuse prevention programs do a better job teaching

certain students. Pretest results suggested that students who knew the least about maltreatment were male, had mothers with less education, were not white, and lived with two parents. The evidence suggests that, overall, students with two parents and who were Asian learned the most. Although the self-report data show gains among all groups, interviews indicate that black and Hispanic students may not have been reached effectively. Certain cultural groups may also find particular parts of the curriculum unfamiliar. For example, several recent Southeast Asian immigrants reported difficulty with the idea of disclosing about their parents.

Impact on Adolescents, Parents, Schools, and Communities

There was no evidence that students who took these classes disclosed abuse more often or actually used the skills they were taught to protect themselves. The CAPTA legislation directs programs to supply students with follow-up opportunities to disclose abuse. In almost all programs, students are expected to report to adults. Unfortunately, students stated that they were more likely to report being abused, but still not comfortable talking to an adult when disclosing. Evidence from other life skills programs indicate that "behavioral intent" may not be related to adolescents' actions to avoid smoking or to prevent pregnancy (e.g., Cleary, et. al. 1988; Kirby 1984). Therefore, even the students' qualified intent to disclose may not result in real, desired behavioral change. The absence of any reports in this sample may be attributable to chance but if it is not, it confirms our concern that youth did not learn skills to disclose. (By chance alone, if 2 percent of the sample is being abused or has been sexually abused, we would have expected nine reports.)

The identification and reporting functions of CAPTA programs can be improved. Many students reported that they did not feel they were able to disclose without their friends finding out. Most students stated that they still did not feel as comfortable disclosing to a professional as they did to a friend. Students' limited knowledge of community resources suggests that they would face considerable difficulty in identifying ameliorative services in the event they were abused or becoming abusive.

Satisfaction

Students and parents reported a favorable experience in high school CAPTA programs. Generally, students thought the CAPTA curricula were valuable, and reported that they thought they were more able to protect themselves. Parents also reported that they supported the programs. There was no evidence that the overall impact of high school–level CAPTA programs on students and their families was harmful. Neither students, their parents, nor local professionals reported any negative effects. The strongest concerns came from a few parents who were worried that CAPTA might go "too far" in teaching adolescents to turn in their parents, and from CPS and law enforcement professionals who felt that CAPTA staff sometimes were too zealous in the interviewing of students and the reporting of disclosures.

Recommendations

Recommendations are based on the study findings and on a broader understanding of effective prevention programs for adolescents. Child abuse prevention specialists can find satisfaction in the findings that the prevention program is well liked by students and increases their knowledge about adolescent abuse. Yet there are many reasons to consider ways to improve the adolescent program. The recommendations that follow are provided in that spirit. In this chapter, recommendations are offered about ways to improve on the current curricula and classroom and visitor-delivered approach to meeting the CAPTA goals. Then, in chapter 6, recommendations are forwarded regarding ways to achieve a desirable refocusing of child abuse prevention programs away from singular reliance on classroom approaches toward school and community-based approaches. Suggestions for procedures that would be likely to lead to more coordinated and effective child abuse prevention programs are tendered.

Program Goal and Focus

Preventing the victimization of adolescents is a worthy goal that requires the continued commitment of significant resources. Adolescents who are being abused currently receive little attention from child welfare services unless they are already in foster care. Although few services are available for adolescents, they should be informed of their rights and opportunities for escaping victimization. The relative lack of services for youth fifteen years of age or older causes other difficulties for high school child abuse prevention programs that are not witnessed in programs for younger children.

Getting Help

Although "reporting" or "disclosing" are considered important goals of child abuse prevention programs, the most basic goal is to protect children and youth. Age fifteen is near the top of the child abuse and reporting spectrum—few intrafamilial child abuse events begin and few new reports come in after that. In many jurisdictions, a fifteen-year-old youth who reports her or his victimization by a family member would not receive services beyond perhaps a preliminary investigation—the child welfare system is increasingly aimed at rescuing the youngest and most helpless children. So, neither primary prevention nor early intervention by agencies of intrafamilial child abuse are likely to result from these programs. Child abuse prevention programs must recognize these constraints and help adolescents find sufficient support from the limited resources available in order to avoid further victimization. On one hand, adolescents should not be given unrealistic notions of the extent of response that they might receive from a disclosure. On the other hand, prevention specialists should also be careful that such areas of real concern such as emotional abuse not be under emphasized merely because the protective service system is unlikely to respond to emotional abuse cases. Adolescents may need guidance and practice in how to respond effectively to various forms of family dysfunction and parental assault or neglect.

California's enabling child abuse prevention legislation mandates that children be taught how to disclose and obtain help, and that they receive safe and private opportunities for reporting at school. Presenters can further increase the likelihood that students are comfortable and knowledgeable about contacting community resources, not only immediately after programs, but on an ongoing basis. Students should be able to identify themselves to a professional without their friends or peers ever knowing that they did. Child abuse prevention presenters, high school staff, and peer counselors (as parts of school-based SCAN teams) should be well-trained regarding reporting procedures. For example, at the end of class some programs did not provide every student with a card that they must turn in to the teacher as they leave the class. Thus, students who might have wanted to make an appointment to discuss a victimization experience might not have because of concern they would be singled out by classmates.

Better still, some municipalities have also developed warmlines for children and youth. One developed by The Pebble's Project (a child abuse prevention agency in Austin, Texas) is peer administered and now in its fourth successful year. Students can call anonymously with a range of concerns, including child abuse. The availability of such a confidential means to discuss victimization at any time is far preferable to the very limited opportunities for discussion that follow visitor-delivered presentations.

Teacher-delivered curricula given over a relatively long-term period may more effectively foster disclosure and other forms of help seeking. Health and family life educators are the most likely presenters of material about adolescent abuse and acquaintance rape. Typical health and family life curriculum last a semester (roughly eighteen weeks) during which students typically discuss dating, drinking, reproduction, sexually transmitted diseases, and numerous other topics that promote students' ability to frankly discuss various ways that life confronts students (and what they can do about it). As a result of both planned and incidental activities that promote student trust in their teacher, many family life educators hear from students about pregnancies, diseases, and substance abuse problems. We expect that they would certainly hear more about child abuse if it were discussed by them in an integrated instructional program.

But, the skeptical reader might ask, are teachers really able to deliver such charged content and to discuss the likely aftermath of reporting and ways that it relates to the complex child welfare service system? That is, would teachers know what to say to a student who asked, "If my friend was being abused and she called the child abuse hotline what would happen to her?" Many teachers would not initially know how to respond. They could learn quite readily from consultation with a child abuse prevention specialist. According to the PPS administrators, many CAPTA instructors were trained quickly. Family life educators faced and overcame the same quandary regarding talking about AIDS-infecting practices. Indeed, given the often distant relationship found in this study between child abuse prevention specialists and child welfare service providers, adolescents are not now provided with much information about the likely outcomes of a call to CPS. This may just be local to California, but we expect that our finding of very limited communication between community-based child abuse programs and public child welfare agencies would be an accurate characterization of many areas.

Also more flexible are school-based SCAN teams that include staff, administrators, pupil personnel service providers, and teachers and, thereby, offer multiple points and places of contact for adolescents who need to discuss their experiences. Because students told us they feel more comfortable talking with peers, a well-trained, ongoing peer counselor program might well also serve to promote disclosures or help seeking.

The California legislation is clear, and rightly so, that its goal is not only to promote disclosures of abuse by students. In keeping, we are not judging the high school child abuse prevention program by this account. Indeed, if the high school program were the *only* California program, there might be more disclosures of abuse at the high school level. It is possible that some abuse victims were identified as a result of presentations received in junior high school. Project Pebble in Austin, Texas, reports as many as hundred adolescents disclosed abuse following their presentations in a single school district! Yet the point of child abuse prevention programs for adolescents is not, primarily, to detect reportable child abuse. By age fifteen, most youth who will be abused have been abused and most who will report have reported. Further, if they do report to formal child welfare services they will receive little redress. The content delivered to adolescents generally focused on preventing acquaintance rape and assault. The goal of these programs most appropriately is to help youth to minimize exposure to situations that might lead to assault, effectively handle those that are threatening, and seek help when they cannot protect themselves from assault.

High school child abuse prevention programs emphasize the prevention of acquaintance rape of girls and sexual abuse of girls. The curriculum should emphasize that both boys and girls are potential victims and perpetrators of child maltreatment and other forms of family violence. In fact, all forms of maltreatment, including psychological maltreatment, physical abuse, and neglect, should be included in each curriculum. Instead of only emphasizing those forms of abuse that receive the most public and media concern, such as sexual abuse and severe physical abuse, adolescents also need to know about responses to less dramatic but more common forms of abuse experienced daily by many teens. These more common forms include gang violence, drug-related harassments, interpersonal violence between peers, and emotional abuse and neglect from adults. Because classroom child abuse prevention programs are already crowded with topic areas, emphasis on the specifics of these additional areas is not feasible. More emphasis on common themes of helping potential victimizers to recognize their right to be safe, their right to get help, and on the provision of peer and professional resources to help youth at school should be the common content of programs. Classroom presentations with these simple themes could be readily delivered with the remaining resources devoted to developing helping resources.

Specific instruction related to acquaintance rape should be revised. Although this topic is considered important by students, parents, and providers, it was not learned very well by students. The content fits more closely with content related to dating and avoiding or diffusing potentially abusive situations, which is consistent with the intent of conventional family life and health education courses. Instruction to prevent acquaintance rape—and other assaults—requires significant rehearsal of strategies. This is currently not possible in the brief child abuse prevention presentations. Consultation with family life educators to ensure adequate instruction on acquaintance rape is needed. Family life teachers and child abuse prevention instructors must decide together what should be taught to high school students, when, and by whom.

Parent Involvement

Begun with borrowed assumptions that child abuse is the responsibility of malicious parents, child abuse prevention programs often neglect parents. Yet, as discussed in chapter 1, as much as half of adolescent physical abuse occurs because of conflicts stemming from or aggravated by the transition to adolescence. In other words, adolescent abuse may often be the result of parents who are simply unable to more effectively cope with the stress of living with and guiding an adolescent. Current parent involvement efforts are slight and unsuccessful. The typical premise is that parents are entitled to be informed of what their children are learning about abuse. There is no serious expectation to strengthen parenting. Yet, parents actively seek ways to reduce conflict with their children. In addition, whereas primary prevention programs to teach high school students about parenting (e.g., "Positive Parenting") are in place in Utah and other states (Kosta and Moore 1989), tenth graders probably need more assistance getting along with their current parents than their future children. Also, given what we know about the difficulties that adolescents have in projecting themselves into the future, efforts to practice conflict resolution skills in their own families are critical.

Several parent-adolescent communication training programs have been developed and supported by modest empirical evaluations (e.g., Hall 1984). The Nurturing Program for Parents and Adolescents (Bavolek 1988) appears to have the widest adoption and also has been shown to reduce parental belief in corporal punishment, increase knowledge of appropriate strategies in behavior management, and result in parents and adolescents reporting decreased family conflict. Both groups overwhelmingly reported that the program had made a positive impact with their parents or teens, respectively.

The program involves ten three-hour meetings in which the

parents and adolescents begin by working separately to under-stand the unit's concepts. After a break, adolescents and parents join together to role-play the use of the communication and conflict resolution strategies they had earlier discussed. (At first, parents role-play with an adolescent from another family.) Each evening's denouement includes visualization of positive self and family experiences and issuing of individual and family home practice exercises. To date, the program has been structured to invite all comers or has been by invitation to families that school personnel have identified as experiencing considerable strain. In several schools, parents who have complete the course have developed a support group and brought in new parents each semester.

Although the program results in measured reductions in the program author's measure of abuse potential (the Adolescent/Adult Parenting Inventory) the evidence is not clear that this program reduces adolescent abuse. What is clear, is that some very troubled families that are at risk of adolescent abuse have participated in the program and they indicate that the experience is important. Even within the classroom-based, visitor-delivered models of child abuse prevention such a program is feasible. As with the current adolescent-only approaches, child abuse preven-tion specialists could operate such groups under the auspices and roof of the school. Such programming should be available at least in every high-risk high school.

Integrated Adolescent Child Abuse Prevention Training

A more effective and efficient way to provide a comprehensive adolescent prevention program to adolescents would be to better coordinate and integrate the currently fragmented prevention ef-forts now underway. Too much is expected from outside agency-provided, classroom-based child abuse prevention programs. Many other prevention efforts and professional resources exist outside of the child abuse community; child abuse prevention programs should be integrated with other prevention efforts along several dimensions.

Services to children and youth of all developmental stages should be integrated. High school CAPTA programs should be part of a careful sequence of child maltreatment prevention approaches that run from preschool through senior high school. Content and instructional approaches should be first introduced at the time students are developmentally ready for them, and then reinforced and expanded appropriately through the higher grades. Although now attempted in various ways by local programs, this effort should be organized at the state level to implement comprehensive curriculum at all school levels. In California, coordinating child abuse programs with the State Department of Education's efforts to develop a comprehensive K–12 health curriculum and plan for health services in the school offers an ideal opportunity to incorporate child abuse into a model curriculum for drug and alcohol prevention education and AIDS prevention and control (California State Department of Education 1989). The initiative emphasizes the "spiraling and articulation" of prevention concepts so that key prevention concepts receive early introduction and increase the scope and complexity of the presentation as students continue through school. Although not currently designed to address child abuse, the initiative promises an infrastructure in the schools that supports a comprehensive program of health promotion from kindergarten to graduation.

A comprehensive K–12 child abuse prevention curricula should not be designed in isolation from other intended prevention curricula. Some child abuse prevention program providers have assumed a broad mandate of reducing victimization of vulnerable peoples; for example, some programs focus on battering (Levy 1984). If such a broad definition of program goals is widely adopted, then resources must be fastidiously managed and efforts at the state and local levels to prevent the abuse of various populations of vulnerable people carefully coordinated. Some child abuse prevention programs and many family life education programs now include this content, but it is not clearly endorsed or organized. An assessment of current teacher-delivered instruction to prevent child abuse and family violence should be undertaken in order to enhance the linkage between child abuse prevention and school district programs. Adolescent abuse is conceptually a bridge between the various forms of child abuse and the forms of family violence that occur in adulthood, including abuse of spouses and the elderly (Garbarino, Schellenbach, and Sebes 1986). Therefore, high school–level health and family life classes may be appropriate places to introduce subject material on all forms of abuse across the life span.

Efforts to teach child abuse prevention to high school and younger students should be coordinated with other life skills approaches to enhancing health and welfare. Life skills approaches to prevent substance abuse, smoking, pregnancy, AIDs, and school dropouts are ubiquitous in America's high schools. Training in assertiveness, self-control, positive self-talk, managing peer pressure, and help seeking should not be taught separately by prevention experts in each area. Helping students to change their world view and their behavior is very difficult, and achievement of these goals will not happen without tight orchestration of teaching efforts. The local public school system is the only sensible choice for coordinating prevention content from smoking to child abuse in kindergarten to high school.

A Conceptual Guide to a K–12 Child Abuse Prevention Curriculum. A comprehensive, integrated K–12 child abuse curriculum can be produced at the state level and disseminated to local schools as guidelines for instruction. As will be discussed further, the role of the prevention specialist in the designing and teaching of a K–12 curriculum may well involve more consultation than direct provision of services.

First, children and youth should be taught about prevention topics beginning at a time in their lives when they need protection in those topic areas, but not before they are developmentally ready to safely use the skills, attitudes, and knowledge they are taught. We know, for example, that toddlers are at some risk for neglect, emotional abuse, physical abuse, and sexual abuse. We also know that they cannot yet be expected to use skills, attitudes, and knowledge to protect themselves. Clearly, knowledge derived from research in child development is necessary to instruct prevention specialists on when to introduce various topic areas to children.

Many issues need to be identified and considered carefully.

Some issues have to do with potential risks involved in teaching topic areas too early. For example, after what age are children ready to hear that their own parents or caretakers are the people most likely to abuse them, without the risk that these children will suffer unnecessary fear and withdrawal from their customary primary sources of love and affection? Or, at what age are children ready to be taught verbal and physical self-defense techniques without putting them in greater danger of being harmed by the potential abuser?

Other issues have to do with the dangers associated with teaching topic areas too late. Given the fact that preadolescents can be raped by their peers or older children, should we wait until high school or even middle school to began talking about acquaintance rape? Or, can potential sex offenders and potentially violent individuals be reached or even identified and helped at very young ages through programs that discuss simple aspects of parenting and caretaking?

A second guideline is that the efficiency of prevention efforts can be maximized by identifying common key elements of prevention curricula, teaching them in achievable and incremental steps, and reinforcing them through the developmental stages. Therefore, objectives for any program taught at any level should be realistic for most of the children being targeted. In addition, once a topic is introduced at a developmental level, it should be reinforced as the child matures, although at gradually more sophisticated and complex levels. Learning theory strongly suggests that such steps would maximize the desired results.

The efficiency of prevention efforts can also be maximized by identifying and teaching common elements in age-appropriate fashion. Table 5–1 offers a matrix of topics and content for caregivers and children to learn. Many of the health and family life issues that are being introduced into school prevention curricula today contain common key elements. Table 5–1 represents a beginning framework of how two series of core concepts, one for caregivers and one for children and youth, can be taught in an incremental, gradually more sophisticated series of topics throughout the K–12 years. Sensitivity to the needs and rights of vulnerable people is a common key element of curricula related

Table 5–1

Matrix of Topics on Child Abuse Prevention

Target Population	Core Concept	Preschool	Elementary	Middle/Jr.	High School
I. Caregivers of Children and Youth (Includes parents and teachers)	Build trusting relationship with children	Support and Listen empathy	Support and Listen empathy.	Letting go and setting limits	Fostering independence.
	Identify symptoms of abuse and reporting	Nonverbal and verbal cues Build basic trust	Foster direct communication.	Talking about sex, dating, baby-sitting	Talk about realities of parenting.
	Self-identification as potential abuser and getting help.	Physical/sex abuse and neglect, failure to thrive substance abuse.	Emotional abuse, personal traits and family history, substance abuse.	Examine own adolescence, examine reaction to child substance abuse.	Reactions to child's lovers and children.
	Positive alternatives to abuse caregiving	Child development/ Time Out/ Redirecting/Beh. Therapy Assertiveness Healthy touch	Child development/ Time Out/ Redirecting/Beh. Therapy Assertiveness Healthy touch	Negotiating fostering independence/ Communicate assertiveness	Establishing life-long relationships.
	Organizing positive recreational/social opportunities for young people	Age appropriate interactions with peers.	Age appropriate interaction with peers.	Social events: dances and sports.	Social events Teen parent functions

(continued)

Table 5–1 (continued)

Target Population	Core Concept	Preschool	Elementary	Middle/Jr.	High School
	Modeling and fostering responsibility in youth.	Caring for the earth, pets and plants.	Caring for the earth, pets, plants, and peers.	Provide baby-sitting training.	Sponsor peer-couselors Adopt-a-grandparent Big bro/sis
II. Children and Youth	Asertiveness/ Enpowerment	Say what you want and don't want.	Dealing with peer pressure.	Communicate with dating partners and other others.	How to help to empower others as well as
	Self-esteem building	I am special	Supporting each child's individual strengths soc/acad/art	Suporting positive peer-interactions	Supporting career/life goals
	Rights	Safe strong free	Safe strong free Victims not guilty	Peer-abuse victim not guilty/ freedom intimidation-gangs, peers.	All dependent people, including elderly, and child abuse have rights.
	Definitions of abuse	Define phy/sex child abuse and child love. Boy and Girl both victims.	Define emotional abuse; examine legal definitions.	Legal definitions of how system works. Define acquaintance rape.	Define forms of family violence/ How CPS system works
	Self-awareness	What do you feel	Body awareness	Good touch/Bad touch	Healthy sexuality/ Homophobia

Target Population	Core Concept	Preschool	Elementary	Middle/Jr.	High School
	Caring for others	Rules about touching and words.	Sensitivity to other's feelings/What's caring.	Baby-sitting younger sib. Caring for dating partner.	Preparenting/What's a healthy family Alternatives to abuse
	Self-protection	Say no/Go tell peers.	Who can abuse/Say no Tell peers, older children, and adults	Who can abuse/Anticipate and avoid danger/including acquaintance rape.	Anticipate problems Physical protection skills/spouse abuse.
Helping others/community agencies/alternatives to CPS system.	Getting help	Tell parent *and* teacher (or other).	Secrets Community agencies Dealing with	abusive parents, caretakers.	Helping a friend/community agencies/alternatives to CPS system. Dealing with abusive parents and caretakers.
	Taking responsibility	Self-control.	Anger-management	Recognize and get help/Relaxation stress reduction.	Recognize strengths and weaknesses/Get counseling. Self-help alternatives.

*In order from highest priority (top) to lowest (bottom).

to child abuse prevention, spouse abuse prevention, acquaintance rape and violence prevention, and prevention of abuse of aging populations. Assertiveness skills are a common key element taught in programs designed to prevent such diverse dangers as AIDS, pregnancy, child abuse, and substance abuse. Self-esteem and self-empowerment are seen as goals in many different prevention efforts. Ways may be developed to teach such simple but basic key elements safely to very young children in attainable, incremental steps, and to older children in gradually more sophisticated ways.

A third guideline is that children and youth learn not only in the formal classroom, but also by doing and emulating, particularly when the learning is related to real life and is an enjoyable activity. Instead of taking place only in fragmentary and occasional classes, prevention skills, attitudes, and knowledge should be continually reinforced through informed guidance of children and youth in all their social interactions in school. Prevention theory and strategies should be taught to all school personnel and be used on the playground, in the physical education class, and in the lunchroom. A teacher can make a lasting impression on children by dealing effectively with a bully and his victim in front of the swings at recess. In other words, all school personnel who work with children have opportunities to teach and *model* desired skills, attitudes, and knowledge. The selection and training of teachers and other school personnel are therefore important elements to any school-based prevention program. As discussed above, these teachers should reflect the diversity of the students they serve.

A fourth guideline is that peer pressure and the influence of older children on younger children can be used effectively in prevention efforts. Peers and older children or youth can be prepared to instruct and guide targeted student populations. Informal and formal student counseling systems can be constructed that benefit not only the targeted populations but the student counselors themselves. Again, these student counselors and teachers should reflect the diversity of the students they serve.

A fifth guideline is that the latest knowledge of teaching methodologies should be employed. The skills, attitudes, and knowledge taught should reflect not only the developmental level of the target population of students, but what is currently known from research.

A sixth guideline is that teaching methodologies should employ language and techniques that are likely to work well with the student population served. They should be sensitive to language differences, differences in cultural and familial expectations, and differences of gender, for example.

Given these guidelines, the K–12 curriculum should contain learning objectives, teaching methodologies, and evaluation strategies for each grade level. At each grade level, intended skills, attitudes, and knowledge should be introduced in each of three general content areas; prevention of abuse of children by adults and much older children, prevention of abuse of children by their peers, and prevention of children becoming abusive to other, more vulnerable people.

Prevention of abuse of children by adults and much older children will contain much of the now traditional "say no, go tell" content in the early grades. Younger children can also have self-esteem, empowerment, and assertiveness reinforced. As children develop, they will become ready to consider the more complex issues related to defining emotional abuse, understanding that both heterosexual and homosexual rape occurs and needs to be reported, and understanding that both boys and girls can be victims or offenders.

Prevention of abuse of younger children by their peers will have to relate to dealing with bullies and wimps, playing doctor, and such key elements as assertiveness, self-esteem, and empowerment. Soon, many children will be dealing with increasingly complex social issues in their lives such as gangs, peer pressure, drugs and alcohol use, and dating.

Prevention of children becoming abusive themselves also can begin with young children. The dynamics of passivity, aggression, and assertiveness can be learned through the kinds of social interactions even very young children experience with each other. Again, as they mature, children will become ready to consider how they relate to their younger siblings, the children they babysit, and, eventually, their own children. Indeed, preparenting skills can be taught throughout the grades through consideration of the dynamics that the children have with more vulnerable people in their lives. Children should be taught not only how not to abuse others, but how to care for, empathize with, and protect others.

The Future

Child abuse prevention programs were designed to fill a vacuum of information about child abuse in the preschools, elementary schools, and middle schools. Less of a vacuum exists at the high school level, as nearly 80 percent of our youth will receive family life education or health education that includes at least some content on sex education and self-protection that may overlap with CAPTA training (Kenney, Guardado, and Brown 1989). Whereas instruction about acquaintance rape and child abuse provided in these classes should be strengthened, at least the requisite structure and staff are available to teach it. As states develop complete a K–12 health curriculum, public school students will be reachable through health education classes. This curriculum could and should help to prevent child abuse. A coordinating and consultative approach is warranted at the high school level. Child abuse prevention staff would have opportunities to have greater impact and their abilities and experience would be more efficiently used. This must occur if our growing student population is to be adequately served. But the issue is more than a budget issue. The larger question is: What do high school students need and when do they need it? The currently configured child abuse prevention program offers some of what they need—content on acquaintance rape and sexual abuse—but does not offer it as early as students need it. That is, the current K–12 approach provides information across the school years, but fails to offer a coherent and consistent approach to self-protection and the on-site staff to implement it even when class is out.

California's high school program was pioneering, but the current structure of the high school programs does not appear to be the best way to meet the legislation's dual intent to "prevent the occurrence of child abuse" and "reduce the general vulnerability of children (State of California, Assembly Bill 2443, 18975.7)." The field of prevention is moving beyond the model of brief classroom presentations to students. In other states, exemplary programs are endeavoring to prevent the victimization of adolescents by working to change the ecology of the school and community environments so that adolescents are schooled in safer environments (Bernard 1989; Kean 1989; Kennedy Foundation 1988). The current approach is not likely to build the ability of schools to prevent child abuse because that is not its focus. Child abuse prevention presenters visit high school classes for about two of the four-thousand hours that our youth spend in high school. Our adolescents need more constant and school-wide support in their efforts to avoid being victimized or victimizers. Child abuse prevention programs in California and other states should transcend conventional implementation strategies and strive for a school-(not classroom) centered and teacher-(not visitor) led approach.

Revise the Role of Prevention Specialists

To increase coordination, the role of high school child abuse prevention providers should change. The staff of child abuse prevention programs should gradually take a more consultative role, working to share and then transfer the primary responsibility for direct teaching of the programs to teachers in the high schools. Ideally, the enthusiasm and creativity of the child specialists would be preserved in such a model. Another advantage of an approach that provides consultation to existing high school teachers is the training those teachers have in teaching adolescents. Many family life educators have vast experience and excellent rapport with students. This is unique among the high schools—health and family life education staff are not common in the earlier grades. High school child abuse prevention programs should use this excellent opportunity to offer consultation on child abuse. Relieved of some of the responsibilities to present content to students, child abuse prevention efforts on behalf of high school students could move toward whole school and community-based efforts rather than only classroom-based curricula. As indicated earlier, staff responsibilities would include the facilitation of adolescent protection teams in the schools. Staff responsibility would include the provision of training and consultation about child abuse to high school teachers, other professionals, and parents. With an anticipated reduction in the number of student contact hours required of child abuse prevention staff, the salaries and opportunities of staff would increase, thus perhaps reducing the current high turnover.

Planned variations of the classroom-level, visitor-delivered child abuse prevention should be tested. The small to modest gains from the current approach indicate that alternative approaches could be attempted without unduly risking the welfare of adolescents. Variations that deserve testing include efforts to enhance the capacity of teachers to present about child abuse, work with student conflict managers or peer counselors to be resources to other abused youth, and SCAN or APT teams. Because most high school programs focus on peer-to-peer abuse, approaches that increase the capacity of the school and students for conflict containment and caring seem especially promising. In California, like many other states, funds for child abuse prevention flow from children's trust funds directly to community-based child abuse prevention agencies without comment or access by state departments of education or local schools. Allowing schools to compete equally with community-based organizations for child abuse funds would enrich child abuse variations.

6
Toward More Efficient Prevention

U niversal adolescent abuse prevention programs must be justified by their results. Our results do nothing to disconfirm
the conclusions of Reppucci and Haugaard (1989):

> Preventive interventions for school children have much appeal
> because of their potential both to reach large numbers of
> children in a relatively cost-efficient fashion and to reduce the
> number of children affected by sexual abuse. However, having
> positive goals is not enough. Effectiveness of intervention is
> critical. Yet most programs appear to continue on the
> strength of their positive goals rather than on a systematic
> evaluation of their effectiveness (p. 1268).

The effectiveness of universal, visitor-delivered, classroom-based
high school child abuse prevention programs is still not certain,
although it seems that even the best of these programs are unlikely to achieve their goals.

Difficult decisions about efficient strategies for preventing
child abuse have generally been avoided. Relying on the false
notion that child abuse is equally distributed across the population and the somewhat more valid concern that targeted child
abuse services may be stigmatizing, decision makers have chosen
to provide universal child abuse prevention services whenever
possible. In the United States, at least, this has been not been
deemed possible for more expensive programs like perinatal public health visitor programs. To be universal, programs must be

convenient and low cost. Brief classroom presentations fit that description. For high school students, at least, such programs appear to increase knowledge, desired attitudes, and intended skills. Yet, theory and experience suggest that this is not sufficient to make a real difference in their lives.

At the high school level, universal classroom-based programs will not effectively *prevent* child abuse by adults. They are too late for that. At best, they prevent the continuance of the relatively few cases that have onset in the high school years and increase *detection* of abuse that had previously occurred. If astutely delivered, high school programs could deter the abuse of adolescents by their peers as well as divert some adolescents from eventually abusing children. Although we did not see evidence of this in our sample, we have heard third-hand reports that many disclosures of abuse may follow presentations to high schoolers. These reports were followed by referral to a support group. This is an important contribution to the well-being of young people, but does not require child abuse prevention specialists. Health and family life educators are well equipped to help youth detect abuse and to give them information they need to get help. High schools can set up peer counseling programs to help facilitate disclosures.

Child abuse prevention programs may help prevent acquaintance assault, although the brief format and our results suggest that the desired effect is small or absent. As long as universal programming spreads assault prevention resources so thin, this is unlikely to change. Researchers in the United States (Conte and Schuerman 1987) and abroad (Gough 1988) have concluded that child abuse prevention programs may most often be provided for those children who are already the best protected by their skills and their families. This confirms the description of allied classroom-based prevention programs (Snow, Gilchrist, and Schinke 1985). Universal programs correct this form of inequity, but fall short by providing the same service regardless of need. The mismatch between program effectiveness and need raises troubling questions about the appropriateness of an approach that misses the most alienated and at-risk youth.

The American Psychological Associations' Task Force on

Promotion, Prevention, and Intervention Alternatives concludes that:

> (s)uccessful programs have a number of common features including *careful targeting of the population* (emphasis added), the capacity to alter life trajectory, the provision of social support and the teaching of social skills, the strengthening of existing family and community supports, and rigorous evaluations of effectiveness (p. 57).

Universal classroom-based prevention are not carefully targeted, do not offer much social support, do not strengthen existing family and community supports, and have not been justified by evaluation. This concluding chapter reviews prevention alternatives that might protect adolescents from abuse and do so at an acceptable cost.

Classroom, School-Level or Community-based Child Abuse Prevention?

The fundamental assumption of classroom-centered child abuse prevention programs as they are typically delivered is that work at the level of the individual (i.e., the child) is the first and foremost course of action. This assumption harkens back to a time when individuals were the center of child abuse research and practice. Child abuse was explained by looking for psychopathology in the abuser and abuse-proneness in the victim. In theory, child abuse was solved by teaching the victim to resist, by reporting the abuse, and by punishing the abuser.

This concern with the personal characteristics of the abuser and the abused was slowly expanded to include high-risk interactions between parent and child (Bell and Harper 1977; Kadushin and Martin 1985) and was finally overshadowed by the concern with the social ecology of child abuse (Garbarino 1976). That is, conceptualizations of the causes and prevention of child abuse have expanded to multiple influences that include parent, child, and the interaction between them; household make-up and resources available to the family; stress and strategies for coping with stress; informal or social support; community services; and cultural and societal values. Classroom prevention efforts do not reflect this progress in thinking.

Although the previous chapter considered ways to improve child abuse prevention content in high school classes—because this can be part of an effective program—we argue that this content should be more broadly delivered throughout the school. We earlier distinguished school-level child abuse prevention from classroom-level child abuse prevention. Basically, *classroom-centered* child abuse prevention programs involve instruction within a classroom by a visitor or teacher like any other content (e.g., science or civics) using an academic lesson plan, some discussion, and maybe some role-play instruction or media. *School-centered* child abuse prevention involves efforts to work with the entire school community to improve the response to children and families in the school community and lower the rate of child abuse as well as raise the quality of response when child abuse occurs. Exemplary programs are endeavoring to prevent the victimization of adolescents by working to change the ecology of the school and community environments so that adolescents are schooled in safer environments (Bernard 1989; Kean 1989; Kennedy Foundation 1988). The intent is to weave the academic content on abuse and acquaintance rape together with more fundamental primary prevention concepts of help seeking, caring for others, and self-protection. At minimum, this involves a coordinated set of classroom-centered presentations by school personnel who are identified as resources to students inside and outside the classroom whether or not they are the child's current teacher. In more comprehensive approaches, schools are seeking to restructure the daily school life to reduce victimization and promote help seeking.

Community-based interventions follow from an ecological model of child abuse and are a logical response from community-based child abuse prevention agencies. Such efforts rely on the capacity of child abuse specialists to go beyond a narrow teacher approach to become program developers and community workers and reach groups that would not otherwise be reached in the school. >

Figure 6–1 shows a conical representation of adolescent abuse prevention services as they might effectively be delivered. At the center of the organization of services are a range of classroom-based approaches. This does not mean that the classroom is necessarily the heart of child abuse prevention, but it recognizes that it now holds a central place in the presentation

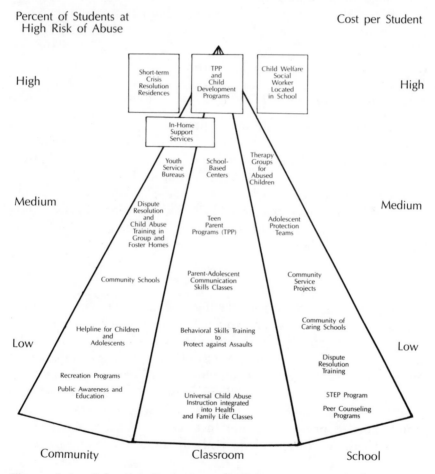

Figure 6–1. *Schematic Depiction of Adolescent Abuse Prevention Programs Across Settings, Risk of Abuse, and Cost per Student.*

of child abuse prevention content. Flanking the classroom programs are school-level and community programs. Within each program locus are a range of potential programs, stacked here to show which are the most general and least costly per student (although not inexpensive when spread across many students) and which are most costly per individual but expected to be most powerful at reducing the risk of adolescent abuse. Each program can be but briefly described here, but the cone suggests the range of programs that could be enlisted in the effort to reduce the abuse-related casualties of adolescence.

Classroom

Child Abuse Awareness Training

As we have discussed child abuse prevention programs rarely go beyond a presentation of information. Given the overwhelming evidence that changing knowledge is *not* a sufficient condition for changing behavior, this strategy is not likely to provide much protection for children. Chapters 2 and 5 describes classroom approaches that have the best likelihood of being effective and argue for the integration of this content into the core health and family life curriculum.

Behavioral Skill Training

When programs include role-playing and active presentation and practice of skills, they are somewhat more likely to have an impact on preventing child abuse. Sheryll Kraizer and her colleagues' *Safe Child Personal Safety Training Program* (Kraizer, Witte, and Fryer 1989) has shown that children can learn and apply some self-protection skills in simulated abduction settings. Muehlenberg and her colleagues have shown skills training can build skills to prevent acquaintance assault. Yet, it is not clear how well these skills work in real situations.

Parent Adolescent Communication Skills Training

As discussed in chapter 5, parent involvement is often an afterthought in adolescent abuse prevention programs. Active parental permission is usually not required to allow students to take the class, but many school districts do provide a chance for parents to come and discuss the curriculum. The chosen times are often in the day and not convenient to parents. Even if they were, parents would not come in significant numbers—and for good reason. Such presentations are about the life and work of the child abuse agency—they are not about the life and work of the parent and child. Little is learned there about parenting (Berrick 1988). Perhaps the most essential step that child abuse prevention programs could take to enhance their effectiveness is to begin making sincere efforts to reach parents whose relationships with their children are troubled and to help build their readiness to get through adolescence. The *Nurturing Program for Parents and Adolescents* (Bavolek 1988) is a good starting point and deserves consideration and adaptation for the varied communities and cultures in which our parents struggle to keep adolescents safe.

Teen Parent Programs

Conventional teenage parent programs probably buffer the long-term risks of abuse by encouraging continuance in school and providing social support. Adolescents in teenage parent programs are typically less isolated and have more support than teens who leave programs. Thus, certainty that the program prevents child abuse is preempted by the alternative conclusion that adolescents with the most resources (and lowest likelihood of abuse) attend teenage parent programs. Still, on the face of it, even brief programs for the best-situated teenage mothers are a good thing. A few programs that provide continuous counseling for as long as three years after the adolescent becomes a mother show additional promise for preventing abuse because adolescents are most likely to abuse after giving birth to several closely spaced children (Brindis, Barth, and Loomis 1987). Such continuous counseling programs reduce repeat births and keep contact with teens beyond the immediate postpartum period. This is the basis for California's Adolescent Family Life Act and is similar to other programs like the Parent Linking Project in New Jersey, which provides free, full-day, on-site child care, transportation, parent education groups, parent-child interaction sessions, individual and family counseling and crisis intervention, and school-based medical services for teens and their children (Pavelec 1989).

Teen Parent Plus Child Development Programs. A few teenage parent programs also offer the opportunity for adolescents to learn to care for children for school credit under the watchful eye of a developmentalist. The School-Age Parent and Infant Development Program in San Diego offers a parenting education class and hands-on experience in the nursery that cares for the children of teenage mothers. Any student can enroll in the child development and parenting class or work in the nursery. A school nurse is assigned to the site on a part-time basis to monitor the well-being of the children. The program has been identified as a model program by the California Department of Education (Brindis and Jeremey 1989). Although not a whole-school program, the Newton, Massachusetts, *Exploring Childhood* program is more than a few classes. The course combines the study of human development in family life education classes with opportunities to work with young children in nearby child-care settings. The full-year course covers a wide range of topics designed to increase the knowledge, skills, self-awareness, and self-esteem of participating students. If more widely integrated into a teenage parent program, this could be a valuable prevention resource to teen parents and future parents.

Classroom-centered approaches do not significantly build the capacity of schools to prevent child abuse because that is not their focus. Visiting presenters visit high school classes for a minuscule fraction of the hours that our youth spend in high school. Our adolescents need more constant and school-wide support in their efforts to avoid being victimized or victimizers. National leadership in the realm of child abuse prevention will be assumed by states that transcend the typical implementation strategy and achieve a school-centered, (not classroom-centered) teacher-delivered (not visitor-delivered) approach. California is at times looked to as a leader deserving emulation. In this case, California's program should be viewed as a trial balloon that other states can learn from.

To date, those who are betting their resources on classroom life-skills training as a preventive intervention are not riding a sure thing. Some approaches to life-skills training slightly increase the odds of success with specific problems like early smoking, but the evidence suggests that life-skills training without simultaneous school and community programs to reach high-risk families does not necessarily effect a difference. Life-skills training programs are developing because of the recognition that the three Rs are very difficult for our troubled children to master and, even if mastered, are not sufficient to help them cope with their environments. Yet, we are in danger of repeating the same error by going the academic route to teaching life skills to troubled children. Such a strategy is likely to miss the same at-risk children whose education, opportunities, and personal well-being are neglected or abused by powerful family, school, and community experiences. We would agree with recent reviewers of child sexual abuse prevention programs and extend their findings to the prevention of other kinds of abuse:

> Sexual abuse education programs aimed at children must be only one, and perhaps a temporary, component of a whole array of prevention efforts that are needed. In the rush to respond to the tragedy of child sexual abuse, many essential preliminary steps in the development of prevention education programs have been ignored or skipped (Tharinger et. al., 1988, p. 631).

Classroom-based child abuse prevention was once pioneering, but no longer appears to be the best way to prevent the occurrence of child abuse and reduce the general vulnerability of children. Current classroom-centered child abuse prevention programs are not principally primary prevention programs because they do not teach skills for reducing child abuse situations or endeavor in a focused way to reduce child abuse risk. Strengthening the capacity of the school and community to prevent child abuse provides a triple resource for the child.

School-Level Approaches

Classroom child abuse prevention approaches have flourished because they are easy to conceptualize and are convenient.

School-level approaches have no abundance of these two appealing characteristics, but neither are they untried. School social workers and psychologists long ago figured out that their efficiency was much greater when they served as consultants to students, teachers, and administrators than when they tried to deliver direct services (Berlin 1962; Chavkin 1985). The limits of teaching individuals to use assault prevention skills when contrasted to reducing the assaultiveness of the environment are rather clear. Less obvious are ways to do the latter. Vandalism and assaults have been reduced by changing the culture of the school (Mayer et al. 1983; Rutter 1979). Programs that have shown success in doing so and that are clearly replicable are described next.

Peer Counseling Programs

Adolescents in our study indicated considerable reluctance about reporting child abuse to presenters from the outside agencies. Youth most often indicated that they would report abuse to their peers. Yet, peers are typically not knowledgeable enough about helping to enhance help seeking. Peer-to-peer counseling programs are growing in number and in the relevance and uniformity of training. Such programs provide an excellent and low cost conduit from student concerns to informal and formal services.

School Transitional Environment Program

Recent research suggests that youth with a social attachment to the school are those most likely to avoid such difficulties as school dropout and misconduct, delinquency, problem drinking, drug abuse, and precocious teenage sexual activity (Comer 1988; Hawkins et al. 1986; Osgood et al. 1988). Whereas classroom life skills training approaches like those employed in conventional abuse curriculum assumes that youth with more life skills will not get in trouble with drugs, alcohol, or acquaintance assault, social attachment theory posits that many young people will experience trouble and that young people with an attachment to school will be able to get help. Classroom-based and social attachment strategies are not mutually exclusive, of course, and the relationships built with family life and health teachers during discussions of the challenges of adolescence can build social attachment.

The School Transitional Environment Program (STEP) has shown much promise for strengthening student's attachment to peers and, especially, teachers (Felner and Adan 1988). The well-evaluated program holds a simple premise: that consistent class-room make-up and teacher contact will change the ecology of the school and give students the chance to develop consistent relationships. Designed to facilitate the transition to junior or senior high—but also used for continuity through out junior or senior high—the program slightly reorganizes the school day in order to significantly reorganize the student's social system. STEP students are assigned to classes so that all primary academic subjects such as English, math, social studies, and science and homeroom are taken with other STEP students. STEP classes are also located near each other (e.g., in one wing or floor of the building). Homeroom teachers also have a different role—they serve as the primary administrative and counseling link between the students, their parents, and the rest of the school. For example, when a STEP student is absent, the homeroom teacher contacts the parents. Each student has a homeroom counseling session every month for about fifteen to twenty minutes. STEP teachers also meet together as a group to offer each other consultation and information.

STEP has reduced a range of social and academic problems among students even when delivered for only one year. A long-term follow up (Felner, Weissberg, and Adan, 1987) on a group of STEP students who received the program in ninth grade shows that they were far less likely to drop out of school; they also had better grades and fewer absences. Findings from a replication study also indicate less depression, substance abuse, and delinquent behavior among STEP students (Felner and Adan 1988). Related findings showed that teachers also improved their attitudes toward students and got to know them sooner and better. Although STEP's impact on child abuse reports or acquaintance assault incidence is not documented, these are the

kind of teacher and teen relationships that foster early and informed action to prevent or end abuse.

Dispute Resolution Training

Community Boards of San Francisco and Project Smart in New
York have provided training to approximately five-hundred
schools to develop dispute resolution or conflict management
programs. The community boards program includes a classroom
curriculum but focuses on the training of students to be conflict
mediators. The program now has many derivatives, but the fundamental components are selecting and training student mediators, structuring elective classes or supervision of the mediators,
and support for the on-site academic coordinators. (The latter
are often pupil personnel services personnel like school social
workers, psychologists, or resource specialist.) A recent study of
the derivative forms of Community Boards' program indicates
that the most successful programs have redundancy in their programs. That is, students learn about conflict mediation in class,
through observation of mediators on the playground and other
settings, through assemblies, and across grades and schools in a
district; with such redundancy, even students who are not
trained mediators demonstrate conflict mediation skill (Gail Kaplan, personal communication, October 30, 1989). At this time,
programs are about equally distributed across elementary, middle, and high schools.

Community of Caring Schools

Over ten years ago, the Community of Caring Schools Program
was developed by the Joseph P. Kennedy, Jr., Foundation to help
provide a comprehensive network of health and social services
for teens in a caring school environment. The Community of
Caring aims to help students postpone sexual activity and prevent adolescent pregnancy by providing a framework in which
all members of the school's community—students, faculty and
staff, parents, and civic leaders—work together to create a caring, supportive environment that emphasizes universal and fam-

ily values and enhances the students' ability to make responsible decisions. The program has been implemented in three-hundred schools and has shown its ability to prevent pregnancies, repeat pregnancies and low birth weight (Joseph P. Kennedy Foundation, 1988). In operation, it has a broader impact on the culture of the school.

The Community of Caring approach emphasizes sharing of knowledge and values and is based on the assumption that caring for parents, teachers, family, and friends is the foundation of a stable life. The curriculum rests on four basic principles: (1) adolescents need to feel deeply cared for if they are to be inspired and influenced by adults; (2) caring means being sensitive and responsive to the many needs of adolescents and includes expressing moral values and ethical principles; (3) the key moral values to be express in a Community of Caring school are those most deeply rooted in family life, namely, the importance of the family itself, love, caring, truth telling, the goodness of sexuality and the value of sexual discipline, the value of school and work, and the importance of planning for the future; and (4) that the life circumstances of adolescents *can* be hopeful. All discussions and activities in the Community of Caring curriculum include ethical reflection and moral teaching. For example, in teaching about drugs, teenagers consider not only their own health and well-being but also their future as founders of strong and healthy families. Discussions and activities address friendship, sexuality, love, and marriage in the light of promise keeping, truth telling, fidelity, honor, and commitment. Moralizing about caring is explicitly rejected in this approach. This is an action-demonstration curriculum and encourages much role-playing of caring actions and service to the community (e.g., by volunteering for Special Olympics).

Community Service Projects

Although Community of Caring schools have not undergone extensive evaluation for the prevention of adolescent assault or abuse, the idea of developing caring through service as a fundamental element of school life offers a sturdy platform for abuse prevention content. Service projects that typify the Community of Caring approach include those recommended by the Carnegie Foundation for the Advancement of Teaching (Harrison 1987) and the William T. Grant Foundation Commission on Work, Family, and Citizenship (1988). Such programs are now mandated to be offered by every high school in Maryland and Vermont. In Atlanta, students must complete seventy-five hours of unpaid service between grades 9 and 11. The Youth Community Service project of The Los Angeles Unified School District is the largest program of all and now operates in twenty-two high schools and involves over five thousand students, largely minority, in service. Several evaluations (e.g., Conrad and Hedin 1982; Hamilton and Fenzel 1988) indicate positive effects on social attitudes, social and personal responsibility, and moral reasoning among participants in community service programs. This augurs well for their success in adolescent abuse prevention.

The child abuse prevention curriculum that may come closest to a conflict resolution approach is one under development for middle schools by the Committee for Children (1989) in Seattle. The curriculum operates at the classroom level but the final lesson assists students in designing to develop a school-wide plan to reduce the level of violence in the school. Prior to that, the curriculum helps students to consider strategies for dealing with a range of interpersonal problems like bullying and gangs and provides some information about anger control training and social problem solving. The emphasis on a school-wide plan is not great and misplaced if it only includes students in its design and implementation. The overall effort of the curriculum away from older perpetrator to younger child abuse content and toward peer-to-peer assault is praiseworthy.

Adolescent Protection Teams

Adolescent Protection Teams (APTS) that typically include social workers, school administrators, and other high school staff in every school can identify appropriate places to include child abuse content in the school curriculum; mechanisms for ensuring that students know all they need to know about community resources; strategies for serving adolescents who are not eligible for conventional child welfare services; and training needs of staff. These teams would have a slightly broader role than a conventional SCAN team, which is designed to, above all, offer an initial response to child abuse. The proposed APTs would also attend to the ways that the school environment—both in class and out—promotes a caring environment and helps prevent victimization. The efforts of the APT would address administrative policy and procedures in the school's role regarding the prevention of child and family violence, staff training, involvement of parents and community, quality assurance, and coordination with other health and life skills promotion efforts.

Therapy Groups for Adolescents

Adolescents who report abuse may receive nothing more than a series of interviews if the abuse is not concurrent and, especially, if the perpetrator was not a family member. These adolescents may feel no less shame, anger, or despair than other assaulted youth. School-based therapy groups have proven to be a welcomed resource for assaulted youth. Offered by the Pebbles Project in Austin for the last four years, these groups have been well enrolled, and a significant relief for youth who receive little other assistance for grappling with the aftermath of assault. The concept of school-based therapy groups is not easily accepted because of the potential for stigmatization. But, according to John Boyle who delivered the groups, youth routinely found ways to talk to their friends about the groups in a way that was comfortable, and the strong desire to have the groups was hardly dampened by any shyness about explaining the group's purpose. This conclusion is confirmed by the excellent attendance and waiting lists for the groups. The groups can facilitate this process by helping each youth to develop an explanation of the groups that is comfortable. The state of Texas has recently passed legislation to use money's paid to the state by sex offenders to support an expansion of therapy groups.

School-based Centers

School-based centers to promote adolescent health and development are another emerging component of the educational institution offering opportunities for collaboration. Although often operated by outside agencies rather than the school, these centers establish a local presence in high schools for health and mental health services. More than 95 percent of centers provide assessment and referral to community agencies. Anecdotal reports from staff in a variety of health centers indicate that disclosure of sexual abuse and parental drug abuse is high (Millstein 1988).

Although use of the health centers requires parental permission, most parents request the full range of services offered (Millstein 1988). As the number of school health centers grows, child abuse prevention service providers should be positioned to take advantage of their potential to serve victimized, victimizing, and at-risk youth. Many also participate in family life education programs. Although these centers now serve less than 1 percent of adolescents nationally, they are growing in number.

New Jersey recently established a pilot project that establishes adolescent centers across the most populous parts of that state. The School-Bases Youth Services Program brings together education and human services. As Governor Kean describes the origination of the program,

> (B)efore we began, services were organized in a manner that was convenient for bureaucracies and interest groups. There was a different program with a different address and different funding for every program. That worked fine for everybody but the kids we were trying to help (Kean 1989, p. 829).

As an alternative, New Jersey created twenty-nine one-stop shopping sites across the state so that there was one youth center in every county. Community agencies—including child abuse prevention agencies—manage the centers. Each center provides mental health, information and referral, health and substance abuse services, and recreation. Many provide parenting education for young parents and hotlines.

Child Welfare Services Social Worker at School

Locating child abuse prevention or child welfare services personnel at schools can help provide prevention and early intervention. Colocating social workers in schools with programs for teenage parents and in schools in which a sizable minority of students are in foster care is particularly sensible. The former approach has been well used by the Teenage Parenting Program (TAPP) in San Francisco for many years. The presence of a social worker provides youth teetering on the edge of trouble with the opportunity to get needed public assistance and with the motivation to provide adequate care for their children. Locating social workers in schools so that they can intervene on behalf of adolescents who have themselves suffered abuse is a growing practice since new resources were made available by the Independent Living Skills Initiative (PL 99-272) in 1987. Based on the Foster Youth Services model, this approach seeks to provide teens with corrective educational, personal, and employment experiences so that they can escape the social ecology of abuse in which they lived prior to their entrance into the foster care system. Although the delayed effects of this program on child abuse are not known, adolescents generally report that they are much better off as a result of foster care and Foster Youth Services than they would have been had they remained at home (Barth 1988).

Community-Centered Child Abuse Prevention

Questions must also be raised about the adequacy of school-centered abuse prevention. Just as the field of prevention must move beyond brief classroom presentations, school-centered approaches should also be augmented by community-based strategies. Whereas effective school-based programs can reduce the likelihood of an abusive attempt through outreach to families (not just reduce the possible sequelae of an abusive attempt), the dismal record of schools in reaching parents is a certain liability of this approach. To address the abuse of adolescents, Guerney

(1986) writes, "it becomes apparent that it is at the level of the individual parent(s) that interventions must be focused at this time" (p. 279). That is, conventional classroom and school-level "child abuse prevention" are really aimed at detection and, perhaps, early intervention. Children are thought to stop existing abuse through fighting back or to recognize and report abuse. Yet there are few resources to support them before or after detection of abuse. Primary prevention activities that are family-centered or community-centered are equally needed.

Public Awareness through Media

Adolescents do learn from brief presentations on child abuse. Nationally, public opinion polls and still increasing child abuse reports show strong support for efforts to reduce child abuse. Television campaigns like those of the National Committee for the Prevention of Child Abuse seem especially effective in reaching the public. Church and community center involvement in discussing adolescent abuse are also critical. Such efforts provide a starting point for subsequent instruction.

Recreation Programs

Recreation programs have a long but unpublicized history of involvement in combatting delinquency and child abuse (Jewell 1989). Jane Addams was a strong advocate for the role of recreation in protecting children. She believed that recreation competes with vice and created the first public playground in Chicago that became the model for others throughout the nation (Addams 1909). The community of recreation specialists is increasingly aware that "recreation must serve the disadvantaged, handicapped, and other populations and must strive to achieve significant goals by reducing social pathology, contributing to neighborhood strengths, and building family unity and intergroup understanding (Kraus 1984, p. 122–23). Training that helps identify abused children and understand appropriate responses is now built into the training of recreational specialists.

Of course, few recreation providers are formally trained, and child abuse prevention agencies would do well to provide consultation to recreation program staff on child abuse.

Community Schools

The community school concept is historic and perhaps best realized in Michigan where the Mott Foundation has promoted the development of schools as neighborhood centers. Ideally, community-schools programs involve opening the school to the community for education, recreation, social events, and community improvement activities and organizations. Because of many barriers, this is not always feasible. A more useful way to conceptualize the community-schools approach is by looking at the range of family-school partnerships that can strengthen family capacity to avoid abuse (Pennekamp and Freeman 1988). For example, in an inner city school in Milwaukee, lesser skilled parents of children with a range of social and emotional problems participated in school activities such as playground monitoring, assisting in the classroom, and operating a telephone hotline (Gore 1987). As a result, the parenting skills of the participants showed gradual improvement. Schools that provide weekend recreational opportunities for youth help to prevent abuse by reducing the asocial behavior that may lead to confrontations with parents. An evening and weekend recreation program opened in a tough San Francisco neighborhood was recently credited with sharply reducing the arrests of adolescents for possession and sale of crack. That would also be sure to reduce bruising battles between parents and youth.

Child abuse prevention specialists cannot, working alone, create community schools. But this is not a case of all or none. Holding parent-adolescent conflict resolution programs at school at night is a starting point toward community-school approaches to reducing abuse. The seven-day-a-week, twenty-four-hour-a-day multiple service center school for youth and their families is a bit farther down the path.

Hotlines for Children and Adolescents

Hotlines follow a variety of models and differ in their amount of intervention. Some serve only as a warmline or empathic ear while others actively intervene when they become aware of a problems. The latter may contact a social service agency to investigate child abuse. PhoneFriend, in State College, Pennsylvania (as described in Guerney and Moore 1983), and Kidsline in Elk Grove, Illinois, are two of the pioneering hotlines for children. Kidsline operates all day every day and focuses on all children in crisis. It usually receives calls discussing more serious problems than hotlines that operate only a few hours a day. The common characteristics of successful phone lines include: (1) a profamily philosophy; (2) highly trained volunteers; (3) consultation and support; (4) sensitivity to cultural and language differences; (5) professional backup of volunteers; and (6) close contact with other agencies (Long and Long, 1988). In most jurisdictions, help line volunteers are not mandated to report suspected child abuse, although they may encourage adolescents to report or may—if so guided by hotline policy—choose to report.

A national children's hotline center could provide technical assistance to those in existence to assure and improve the quality of care (Long and Long, 1988). The center would include a hotline that children anywhere can call and, when available, that would help link them to local centers. Although initially organized to provide a resource to latchkey children, hotlines for children and adolescents can help address a range of concerns and responses related to adolescent abuse and acquaintance rape.

Prevention Advisory Councils

On a professional service level, the efforts and expertise of professionals in such areas as law enforcement, the child welfare system, the education system, the churches, the medical community, the mental health system, and the courts should be coordinated and integrated. Such coordination could be appropriately sponsored by the local child abuse councils, which could sponsor prevention advisory councils in each county. Cross-trainings, cooperative efforts in program design and implementation, and community events and advertising would be some of the functions of each council. The councils might include law enforcement, education, and CPS representatives, as well as students and their parents, and meet at least semiannually to oversee prevention efforts in each county.

Dispute Resolution and Child Abuse Training in Group and Foster Care

Although the theory of intergenerational transmission of child abuse is disappointedly imperfect, youth in foster and group homes are still vulnerable to perpetrating and being victimized by peer assault. These youth have received little in the way of modeling of effective conflict resolution skills and often lack interpersonal skills for dating and protection from exploitation. Programs that focus on high risk youth and seek to reduce serious abuse should deliver self-protection and dispute resolution training to youth who are living away from home because of family conflict, mental illness, or an adjudication for juvenile crime. The SHARP Program brings content on child abuse victimization to group and foster homes. The Adolescent Sexual Abuse Prevention Project in Wilmington, Delaware, also offers a curriculum that addresses victim and perpetrator issues in a balanced way and has been well tried in residential programs. Child abuse prevention specialists should collaborate with independent living skills specialists funded under PL 99-272 to incorporate content on abuse into their curriculum.

Youth Service Bureaus

As part of the deinstitutionalization movement of the 1970s, abused adolescents and adolescents in conflict with their parents (but who had not broken the law) were no longer to be cared for along with delinquent adolescents. The substitute service mechanism of community-based youth service bureaus was intended to provide assistance to youth and families before they harm each other. When in place, that is what they do. Mental health professionals in somewhat unconventional agency settings provide consultation, group work, and child abuse screening. Society's failure to adequately fund youth service bureaus (e.g., there are eight funded in California for serving its more than 8 million children) is as horrific as society's failure to provide housing to the deinstitutionalized mentally ill. As Bernard Lefkowitz (1987) describes in his excellent book *Tough Change,* many low-income youth leave homes because their families can no longer afford to pay for their care or provide them with a space for living. These pushed-out youth also warrant help from child abuse and child welfare professionals.

In-Home Services

Intensive therapeutic services that help families redress adolescent conflict have been remarkably successful in reducing the need for out-of-home placement (Fraser, Pecora, and Haapala (1988); Kinney et al. 1988). Although increasingly reserved for families of young children who have suffered neglect or abuse and may need foster care, these programs have been widely and success-fully used as conflict resolution programs for adolescents and families prior to abuse. Child abuse prevention agencies have not tended to host these programs and have, instead, settled for a counseling and school-visiting role. (To their credit, some child abuse prevention agencies have developed innovative in-home service programs for mothers and newborns: e.g., Barth, Hacking, and Ash 1986; Olds 1988). As in-home services technology and training improve, child abuse prevention agencies should join more traditional agencies sponsoring this valuable service on behalf of adolescents.

Short-Term Crisis Resolution Houses

Whether youth are pushed out or leave because of family crisis, they are at grave risk of victimization. It is somewhat ironic that child abuse prevention programs have not become involved in developing alternative domiciles for youth at risk of abuse given that many of their sponsoring agencies have contributed to the development of the network of shelters for battered women. The concept is fundamentally the same—youth also need a place to go to get short-term assistance and to decide what, if anything, will make reunification with their families safe. Communities that look at their child abuse services and find no short-term crisis resolution services should recognize the seriousness of this omission.

Rationalizing Adolescent Abuse Prevention

Broader, integrated school-centered and community-based prevention programs may be initially more complex and costly than narrowly conceived stop and go programs. Available resources will not allow for broader and deeper programs to be generated everywhere. Costs may be reduced if child abuse prevention program efforts are combined with other community prevention efforts, the resources of existing community organizations (such as the church) are enlisted, and if adult and peer volunteers are effectively used. Garbarino (1986) argues that "preventive intervention cannot be casual or half-hearted if it is to succeed" and "realistic strategies may involve focusing attention on one form of abuse as it occurs among one target population, or recognizing that different approaches are needed in different populations" (p. 145). Prevention specialists should take the awkward and difficult step of identifying high-risk settings and targeting child abuse prevention in those areas first.

Schools and communities with high child abuse can be discerned. This information has been little used in targeting child abuse prevention programs because it is assumed that: (1) reports do not adequately reflect incidence; (2) child abuse is evenly distributed across localities; (3) targeted child abuse prevention programs are stigmatizing; and (4) data on the location of child abuse is not routinely collected and could not be readily collected. Chapter 1 suggested that reports of child abuse are more representative of incidence than they are misleading, that child abuse is unevenly distributed, and that the distribution can be known. Although the alternative arguments are not without some evidence and logic, they are not substantive enough to support program design justifying universal prevention as the first or only option.

Community-based adolescent abuse prevention programs could target high-risk schools and communities. This would hardly necessitate stigmatizing schools or communities as abusive places. True, if the preventive approach were only to present classroom presentations on sexual abuse this would erroneously indicate that child sexual abuse only occurred in that community. But, there is clearly precedent to develop school-wide programs to address issues like high dropout rates (via student outreach projects), violence (via conflict resolution programs), drinking and driving (via MADD and SADD programs), and student health (via school-based health clinics). These programs are generally considered assets to a school and community, and if anything, are viewed as too minimal an intervention rather than too invasive an intervention. Schools that develop comprehensive plans to increase the safety and health of their students—and include prevention of child abuse within their plans—will be highly regarded. If school boards were responsible for developing plans for such programs and competing for program funds, then the schools would still be less threatened by such a program and, instead, warmly greet prevention efforts. School- or classroom-based approaches could be offered in a universal level, with community-based programs initiated in selected high-risk areas. In this way, all children would at least receive a minimum of basic knowledge, skills, and attitudes.

Although the social ecological models of child abuse were developed and tested in major university-based research efforts, the models can be applied in local communities. Implementation of school-based child abuse prevention services, although preferable to classroom-based child abuse prevention, can still be improved with targeting. Agencies need information and permission to allocate their resources to do the most good. Every school does not need the same amount of intervention. Nor do they now receive the same amount. Child abuse prevention providers indicate that they present their program to some schools more than once a year, for example. One provider recounted that she goes back to the local teen mother program three or four times a year because the mothers need to hear the content on community resources for child abuse and battering more often.

Using a microcomputer and map with color-coded dots to indicate the location of each case and type of family (i.e., single-parent, AFDC, two-parent, non-AFDC), Ditson and Shay (1984) identified ten census tracks with a report ratio of more than 2 per thousand and two tracks with rations of 2.3 and 4.3 per county. As a result, a community group worked to improve the "web of caring" in their neighborhood (p. 508). They worked to locate key persons in the neighborhood and then let these persons know about the availability of clothing, food, and financial assistance.

A multi-modal approach to identifying high-risk neighborhoods has advantages. Zuravin and Taylor (1987) identified incidence rates for census tracts. Rates within tracts were identified for neglect, physical abuse, and sexual abuse. Like Spearly and Lauderdale (1983) they divided report rates by households with children and found a range from 0 to 71 with an average of 19. They then mapped the incidence using color-coded incidence mapping of census tracts and spot mapping of each incident. The incidence mapping helps identify tracts of particular interest and the spot-mapping assures that high-risk areas within census tracts and crossing the boundaries of tracts are not overlooked. The approach identified areas that were exceptions to the expectation that high risk areas were permeated with poverty. Two of the highest-risk tracts were surrounded by tracts with nearly a 0 incidence rate. Information gathered in this way was used to target a child sexual abuse education campaign to school districts including the highest risk children. Maryland's Social Services Administration used the data to make decisions about where to locate community support centers for teenage mothers. With bussing and magnet schools, school districts do not simply reflect the make-up of the local community. That is, the students in a school might be at more or less risk than the students in a neighborhood. Schools should be treated as the smallest unit for intervention. At minimum, school district personnel should know the reporting profile of the local community.

Efforts to prevent adolescent abuse should be balanced along several key dimensions. The first dimension involves proper emphasis of adolescent abuse prevention and child abuse prevention. Rationalizing abuse prevention requires building programs on the best available epidemiology, child abuse theory, and prevention concepts that clarify which kind of abuse is most preventable and important to prevent. Although we are concerned that adolescents are too often left to their own devices, and are always arguing for better services for adolescents, we would not reconstruct public policy to address adolescents first. The greatest emphasis should be on the protection of young children. We agree with Burton White that "the first priority . . . should be getting a child to his/her third birthday in great shape" (1986, p. 1). The earliest intervention is the best intervention. Garbarino (1986, p. 153) writes, "Based upon existing data and programming expertise, the most likely target for both our efforts to prevent maltreatment and to document our success is the severe physical abuse of children by parents in the first three years of life." (We would differ slightly from Garbarino insofar as we think that child neglect probably results in more deaths than physical abuse.) The recent increase in child deaths due to child abuse (Daro and Mitchel 1989) is one horrific reminder that we are not meeting our responsibilities to the very young and their families in their homes. Homicide is the largest single cause of death for infants ages zero to one; 17 percent of infant deaths due to injury are caused by homicide (Waller, Baker, and Szocka 1989). Clearly, child abuse prevention programs should address this as the highest priority.

The prediction of child death has a growing empirical basis (Daro 1988; Fontana and Alfaro 1987) but is still inexact. This inexactitude works to the advantage of child abuse prevention because the children most at risk of severe physical abuse are also the children who are victimized by neglect, sexual abuse, and psychological maltreatment. Approaches that focus on the highest risk children will also benefit other children. The National Committee for the Prevention of Child Abuse has recently redirected their efforts to reduce "serious" child abuse 20 percent in the coming decade (Deborah Daro personal communication, September, 1989). This accomplishment will require focusing additional resources in high risk communities, schools, and families.

A second dimension examines the extent to which policy should direct prevention efforts at the various forms of child abuse, including homicide, physical, sexual, and emotional abuse, and neglect. Whereas school-based child abuse prevention efforts typically focus on sexual abuse, this is not clearly the greatest risk to girls or boys. Indeed, all forms of child abuse (emotional, physical, sexual, and neglect) can have equally serious negative consequences (Egeland, Sroufe, and Erickson 1983; Finkelhor 1986).

A third dimension involves the balance of community, school, and classroom efforts. Far greater community-level efforts are required, and efforts at the school and classroom levels should be maintained but redesigned to draw on and develop educational resources.

A fourth dimension concerns the balance of universal and targeted programs. Although child abuse prevention agencies should devote the great majority of their efforts to high risk populations, a reduced universal effort should continue through media and universal health and family life education. Several state's children's trust funds, including Texas's, are deemphasizing classroom and school-based child abuse prevention programs and investing heavily in the development of home-based parenting programs for families with preschool children. Although states should develop school-level programs that include classroom presentations on child abuse, this should not draw heavily on the resources of community-based child abuse prevention agencies. These costs and efforts should be assumed by the schools as part of their initiatives to develop healthy, prosocial, and safe students.

No child or youth at any age should be left unaided to be a victim of assault. Efforts to provide information to adolescents about abuse and to develop and refer to relevant and available adolescent services should, of course, continue. Classroom-based interventions that focus almost exclusively on the experience of victims and provide no assistance to address current or potential victimizers will not meet their short- or long-term goals. This call to prevent abuse by building a sense of community and caring should help protect adolescents from each other and foster a capacity to seek and accept assistance from service providers.

The best course is to do all possible to create supportive climates for all adolescents while seeking to enhance services available to adolescents and families at greatest risk of abuse. While balancing these two goals, children and youth at greatest risk of serious abuse should be the primary focus of child abuse prevention efforts. To do otherwise is to allow convention and convenience to dictate public policy and, in so doing, to leave the most vulnerable adolescents the most exposed to becoming victims and perpetrators.

Appendix A
Student Self Report Instruments

CHILD ABUSE PREVENTION QUESTIONNAIRE

Please circle the answer that you agree with most.

1. You are tired of your mother yelling at you. What would you do?

    a. Turn on the television and ignore her.

    b. Tell her calmly but firmly that you don't like her yelling at you.

    c. Scream at your mother and slam the door.

    d. Let her yell and do what she tells you to do.

GO ON TO THE NEXT PAGE.

DO NOT WRITE BELOW THIS LINE UNLESS INSTRUCTED TO DO SO

_____ GROUP _____

SCHOOL _____ TEACHER _____

2. John's new stepfather becomes angry and violent when he drinks. Last weekend, the stepfather slapped John's mother and threatened John. What should John do?

   a. Nothing, because the stepfather usually apologizes after he is sober again.

   b. Hide the alcohol in the house or pour it down the drain.

   c. Try to talk with his mother about the problem. If she won't do anything about it, then he may have to go talk to someone else for help.

   d. John should tell his stepfather to leave his mother alone. If he doesn't listen, he should force him out of the house.

3. A teenage girl has an older brother who kept trying to get her alone. One evening he put his hand up her blouse. He quickly left the room when he heard his mother call him.

   a. The girl shouldn't tell anyone because her brother could get in a lot of trouble.

   b. She should just forget it because it probably won't happen again.

   c. She should tell him to stop.

   d. She should tell him to stop and find someone who can help her.

   e. She should get her boyfriend to beat her brother up.

4. Jim is a seventeen-year-old boy who has few friends his own age. Lately he has been wanting to have sex with a girl he knows who is only nine. What should he do?

   a. Nothing because he's done nothing wrong.

   b. Try not to think about it because the feelings will go away.

c. Keep quiet because he will get in trouble if he says anything.

d. Talk to an adult about it.

5. Your mother and father are always fighting with each other. During the last year, the fighting has grown worse, and they are now yelling at you more, too. You are feeling very upset. What should you do?

a. Get used to it, because it probably won't change.

b. Tell your parents how you feel, or talk to someone else about your problem.

c. Stay out of their way as much as you can.

d. Try to get your parents to stop fighting, and try to keep everything as calm at home as possible.

6. You are an eighteen-year-old girl who lives alone with your three-month-old baby. It seems like the baby cries constantly, and nothing you do seems to help. Last night you started to really feel like hitting your baby, and your anger scared you. What should you do?

a. Try to find someone to talk to because you need some help and understanding right now.

b. Deal with it on your own, because that's how you learn to be a good parent.

c. You should not allow your baby to cry so much because that much crying is not normal

d. You should ignore the crying, regardless of how long it goes on.

7. John is a fourteen-year-old who is very close to his cousin, Martin, who is twenty. Martin told John that the best way for John to learn about sex would be for the two of them to play with each other's genitals. John does not want to.

What should John do?

a. Avoid Martin and act as if nothing happened.

b. Talk with an adult about what happened.

c. Do a few things with Martin, and then tell Martin to leave him alone.

d. Tell Martin he'll beat him up if he even says that again.

Please fill in the blanks. Do not leave any line blank. If you do not know an answer, write "don't know."

8. Name two places you could call if you had been abused.

   a. _____

   b. _____

9. Who are two people you know that you could go to if you had been abused (do not give their actual names)?

   a. _____

   b. _____

10. If a friend told me that her stepfather had felt her breasts, I would:

    a. _____

    b. _____

11. Your sister's boyfriend is pressuring her to have sex. She likes him but is not ready to have sex. What are two things you would tell her to do?

    a. _____

    b. _____

12. In the past, John has hit his girlfriend when he was angry.

Name two things he could do to stop hurting her when he gets angry again.

a. _____

b. _____

13. Bob has been baby-sitting a one-year-old girl for about four months. Over that time, she has not gained any weight, and looks very quiet and tired most of the time. What should Bob do?

a. _____

b. _____

Circle the answer that best describes how strongly you agree or disagree with the following statements.

14. If a girl's parents always tell her that she's no good and don't ever let her talk with friends, they are emotionally abusing her.

| strongly disagree | disagree | agree | strongly agree |

15. If a guy wants sex, he has to pressure a girl.

| strongly disagree | disagree | agree | strongly agree |

16. If a boy is sexually abused by a man, the boy will probably become gay (homosexual).

| strongly disagree | disagree | agree | strongly agree |

17. It's hard for girls to say what they really feel about having sex.

| strongly disagree | disagree | agree | strongly agree |

18. It's difficult for boys to be sensitive and caring with girls when they're expected to be tough and in charge.

    strongly   disagree   agree   strongly
    disagree   agree

19. It's fine for a girl to say what she wants, but the guy should have the final say.

    strongly   disagree   agree   strongly
    disagree   agree

20. If a teenager was abused as a child, there is no point in reporting because it was too long ago.

    strongly   disagree   agree   strongly
    disagree   agree

21. This last year, a father hit his son three times with a belt. Each time he left marks on his son. This is abuse.

    strongly   disagree   agree   strongly
    disagree   agree

22. A forty-year-old aunt decides she wants to have sex with her sixteen-year-old nephew. She touches him in a way that turns him on, and then she has sex with him. This is abuse.

    strongly   disagree   agree   strongly
    disagree   agree

23. Mary often has to miss school because her parents make her take care of her brothers and sisters. This is abuse.

    strongly   disagree   agree   strongly
    disagree   agree

24. One night after a party, a boy punches his girlfriend. He apologizes and says it won't happen again. This is abuse.

    strongly   disagree   agree   strongly
    disagree   agree

25. A teenager is baby-sitting a three-year-old girl. He gets turned on when he helps her change into her pajamas. This is abuse.

       strongly   disagree   agree   strongly
       disagree   agree

26. The same boy (in the last question) puts his hand down the girl's pajama bottoms. This is abuse.

       strongly   disagree   agree   strongly
       disagree   agree

27. A fifteen-year-old girl is supposed to be home by 12:00 A.M., but doesn't get home until 3:00 A.M. The next morning her parents tell her to pack some things and not come home until she can live by their rules. This is a case of neglect.

       strongly   disagree   agree   strongly
       disagree   agree

28. Where can this girl go if she doesn't have friends or relatives to turn to?

---

29. A teenager is more likely to be abused by a stranger than by someone they know.

       strongly   disagree   agree   strongly
       disagree   agree

Bill got together with Lisa at a party. Lisa enjoyed kissing him, but got nervous when he started touching her below the waist. She started to pull away, but Bill thought she was just being a tease and continued. Lisa became frightened and started to struggle. Bill seemed so much stronger. She couldn't stop him from having sex with her.

30. This is a case of rape.

    strongly   disagree   agree   strongly
    disagree   agree

31. Lisa was partly to blame because she led him on.

    strongly   disagree   agree   strongly
    disagree   agree

32. She must have liked it because she didn't make him stop.

    strongly   disagree   agree   strongly
    disagree   agree

33. Jack's father always tells him that he will never amount to
    anything because he's lazy and stupid. This is not emo-
    tional abuse because sometimes his father is very nice to
    him.

    strongly   disagree   agree   strongly
    disagree   agree

34. John had an accident and wrecked his father's car. When
    his father found out, he lost his temper and beat up John.
    This is not child abuse because John deserved it.

    strongly   disagree   agree   strongly
    disagree   agree

PLEASE ANSWER THE FOLLOWING QUESTIONS. THE INFORMATION IS CONFIDENTIAL.

A. Date: _____ B. Birthdate: _____

C. Name: _____

D. Sex: 1 ___ male   2 ___ female   E. Age: _____

F. I think of myself as mostly:

    1 ___ Asian American   2 ___ Native American
    3 ___ Hispanic   4 ___ Black   5 ___ White
    Other 6 _____

G. I live in a home with:

  1 ___ one parent   2 ___ two parents   3 ___ other

H. Have you ever had a class that taught you about any of the following subjects (you can check more than one):

    1 ___ human sexuality   5 ___ date rape
    2 ___ physical abuse   6 ___ emotional abuse
    3 ___ sexual abuse   7 ___ child neglect
    4 ___ protection from assault

I. What is the main source of income in your family? (If a two-income family, you can check two places):

My parents/guardians are not working and receive:

    1 ___ AFDC(welfare)   2 ___ Unemployment
    3 ___ Child support
    4 ___ SSI or Social Security
    5 ___ Workmen's compensation

GO ON TO THE NEXT PAGE.

DO NOT WRITE BELOW THIS LINE UNLESS INSTRUCTED TO DO SO.

_____ GROUP _____

SCHOOL _____ TEACHER _____

My parents/guardians work as a:

6 ___ professional or technical worker (doctor, lawyer, teacher, pilot, etc.)

7 ___ manager/business person (inspector, store or restaurant manager, real estate sales, etc.)

8 ___ clerical or sales worker (bank teller, secretary, department store salesclerk, etc.)

9 ___ skilled worker (foreman, painter, seamstress, etc.)

10 ___ machine worker (mechanic, bus driver, laundry or dry cleaning staff, etc.)

11 ___ service worker (waitress, fireman, policeman, cook, hairdresser, etc.)

12 ___ laborer (gardener, truck driver, factory worker, etc.)

13 ___ farm laborer (farm foreman, migrant worker, etc.)

14 ___ member of the armed services (Army, Navy, Air Force, Marines)

15 ___ don't know

J. What is your mother's education?

1 ___ less than seventh grade

2 ___ junior high school (grades 7, 8, 9)

3 ___ some high school (grades 10, 11)

4 ___ high school graduate

5 ___ some college or technical training

6 ___ college graduate

7 ___ graduate school or advanced professional training

8 ___ don't know

CLASS EVALUATION SURVEY

Circle the answer that best describes how strongly you agree or disagree with the following statements.

A. I learned a lot from the class.

    strongly disagree   disagree   agree   strongly agree

B. The class was boring.

    strongly disagree   disagree   agree   strongly agree

C. We had time to ask questions and discuss.

    strongly disagree   disagree   agree   strongly agree

D. We were told when and where we could talk alone with the speaker or other adults.

    strongly disagree   disagree   agree   strongly agree

E. I felt comfortable with the things we talked about.

    strongly disagree   disagree   agree   strongly agree

F. This information will help me.

    strongly disagree   disagree   agree   strongly agree

GO ON TO THE NEXT PAGE.

DO NOT WRITE BELOW THIS LINE UNLESS INSTRUCTED TO DO SO.

_____   GROUP _____

SCHOOL _____   TEACHER _____

G. I could understand the information.

      strongly   disagree   agree   strongly
      disagree   agree

H. The class will make teenagers worry more than they need to.

      strongly   disagree   agree   strongly
      disagree   agree
                                                  10/28/87

I. I am now less likely to be abused.

      strongly   disagree   agree   strongly
      disagree   agree

J. I am now more likely to tell an adult I trust if I or someone I know is abused.

      strongly   disagree   agree   strongly
      disagree   agree

K. If I were abused, I still would not report it.

      strongly   disagree   agree   strongly
      disagree   agree

L. If you answered strongly agree or agree to the above questions, explain why you wouldn't report.

_____

_____

M. In what grade should this class first be given? Please circle one.

      8th   9th   10th   11th   12th

N. The best part of the class was (Check one):

    ___ video or films
    ___ the presenter
    ___ the discussion
    ___ role plays
    ___ asking questions
    ___ other (explain: _____)

O. Before I had the program, I wished I knew this information about how to protect myself from child abuse.

> strongly   disagree   agree   strongly
> disagree   agree

P. I found the information from the program helpful in preventing child abuse.

> strongly   disagree   agree   strongly
> disagree   agree

Q. I found the information from the program helpful in deciding who I know that might be a victim of child abuse.

> strongly   disagree   agree   strongly
> disagree   agree

Appendix B
Survey of California CAPTA Providers

Contact Person: _____ Phone: _____
Program: _____ County: _____

In order to help us evaluate your high school CAPTA program, we would like you to fill out this questionnaire and return it to us in the enclosed envelope. Please check the topics covered in your high school program.

___ Acquaintance rape
___ Assertiveness training
___ Children's rights
___ Communication skills
___ Dealing with peer pressure
___ Definition and dynamics of child abuse
___ Decision making
___ Emotional abuse
___ Healthy sexuality
___ Helping a friend who is a victim or at risk
___ Homosexuality/homophobia
___ Incest
___ Neglect
___ Parenting education
___ Physical abuse by adults
___ Oppression
___ Self-empowerment

___ Self-esteem
___ Self-identification as a potential offender
___ Self-defense
___ Sexual harassment
___ Sex roles
___ Sexual abuse
___ Stranger rape
___ Touching—good vs. bad
___ Trust your feelings
___ Other: _____.

Now please go back and circle the two or three goals that are most emphasized in your program. The remainder of the questions require check marks and/or short answers.

1. Duration of your program: over___ day(s),___ minutes each day

2. Providers are:
    ___paid staff ___volunteer staff ___both paid and volunteer

3. The actual teaching of high school programs is done by:
    ___project staff ___high school teachers or other staff
    ___other (please specify) _____

4. Number of children taught in any given session: ___

5. Specific self-protection skills taught to children:

    _____

    _____

6. Definition of children's rights if specified: (for example, children have the right to live free of abuse, to have positive self-esteem, etc.)

    _____

    _____

7. Is there a parent meeting? ___yes ___no
    If so, what is the duration? ___

What has been the approximate turn-out of parents? ___

8. Number of high schools served: ___

9. Approximate ethnic composition of all students served:
   ___Asian ___Caucasian ___Black ___Hispanic ___Other

10. Funding:
    ___state ___private ___other (specify:_____)

11. Percent of all students served, by grade level:
    ___9th ___10th ___11th ___12th

12. Our project would be interested in participating further in the Family Welfare Research Group study of CAPTA high school programs:

    ___yes ___no

Appendix C
Telephone Survey for High School Child Abuse Prevention Efforts

Name _____

Title _____

Organization _____

Address _____ Phone _____

Interviewer _____ Date _____

1. Do you have an office that coordinates child abuse prevention efforts in your state?

    a. Yes ____   b. No ____

2. If so, what is its name, purpose, and funding?

3. If not, how are prevention efforts coordinated in your state?

4. Does your state currently have a law or regulation that provides for (or mandates) prevention efforts with the high school population?

   a. Yes ＿＿   b. No ＿＿

   If so, please describe (and ask to have a copy of the law mailed to us, if possible).

5. Does this law specifically call for (if information not given, please ask):

   Parents and school staff workshops with information and training concerning:

   ＿＿ a. Physical and behavioral indicators of abuse.
   ＿＿ b. Postworkshop session techniques.
   ＿＿ c. Community resources.
   ＿＿ d. Rights and responsibilities regarding reporting.
   ＿＿ e. School district procedures to facilitate reporting and apprise supervisors and administrators of reports.
   ＿＿ f. Caring for a child's needs after a report is made.

   Workshops for high school students that contain information and training concerning:

   ＿＿ g. The right of every child to live free of abuse.
   ＿＿ h. How to disclose incidents of abuse.
   ＿＿ i. The availability of support resources and how to obtain help.
   ＿＿ j. Child safety training and age-appropriate self-defense techniques.
   ＿＿ k. A period for postworkshop sessions in a school setting that maximizes the child's privacy and sense of safety and provides a period of time following each child's workshop, or a reasonable time thereafter, for any child who on a voluntary basis may want to individually talk with classroom presenters.

6. Overall, about how much does your state spend on school-based child abuse prevention programs?

a. direct costs _____

b. administration _____

c. total cost _____

7. We are particularly interested in child abuse prevention efforts for high school students in your state. Can you tell me how your state has prioritized serving these four age groups: preschool, elementary, middle school, and high school? (1 = highest priority, 2 = next highest, etc.). Please also estimate annual state expenditures for each category.

Preschool _____ Expenditures _____

Elementary _____ Expenditures _____

Middle _____ Expenditures _____

High School _____ Expenditures _____

8. Has there been a change in the relative emphasis put on preventing child abuse of the high school population over the past few years? If so, please explain what the change has been, and the reasons why the change was made.

Does your state (a) fund, (b) coordinate, or (c) have knowledge of the following types of *high school* prevention efforts?

9. Programs given by high school teachers or by other high school staff in family life or other class settings. If yes, please explain rationale.

a. Fund: 1. Yes ___   2. No ___

b. Coordinate: 1. Yes ___   2. No ___

c. Know of: 1. Yes ___   2. No ___

10. Programs by presenters from agencies outside the school system.

a. Fund: 1. Yes ___   2. No ___

b. Coordinate: 1. Yes ___   2. No ___

c. Know of: 1. Yes ___   2. No ___

11. On television or other media forms (e.g., billboards) aimed for high schoolers.

a. Fund: 1. Yes ___   2. No ___
b. Coordinate: 1. Yes ___   2. No ___
c. Know of: 1. Yes ___   2. No ___

12. Are there other types of prevention efforts (not included in questions 10, 11, and 12)? Please describe.

13. In California, most high school–level prevention programs contain one or more of the following three general subject areas: date rape prevention (abuse by peers), child abuse prevention (abuse by adults), and preparenting education (preparing teens to avoid being abusive when they become parents). Does your state prioritize any of these areas over the others? (1 = top priority, 2 = next, 3 = lowest)

    a. Date rape ___
    b. Child abuse ___
    c. Preparenting ___
    d. No priority
       If so, why? ___

14. With regard to child abuse, is there a prioritization given to prevention efforts with each of the following types? (1 = top priority 4 = lowest priority)

    a. Physical ___
    b. Sexual ___
    c. Emotional ___
    d. Neglect ___
    e. No priority ___
       If so, why?

15. Are you aware of any evaluations that have been done on the effectiveness and impact of any high school–level prevention programs in your state? (Please give name, address, phone).

16. Do you know of any in any other state? (Please give name, address, phone).

17. Are you aware of any plans or impending legislation that will have an impact on prevention efforts with the high school population in your state? If yes, please send.

18. What high school level curricula are used in your state? Estimate the proportion of agencies using each.

Name of Curriculum	*Proportion of Use*
a. _____	_____
b. _____	_____
c. _____	_____
d. _____	_____

19. Are there specific high school curricula that the state supports? If yes, please identify and explain why.

Thank you for your help. (Offer results of the write up of this study at a later date).

References

Addams, J. (1909). *The spirit of youth and the city streets*. New York: Macmillan.

Ageton, S. S. (1983). *Sexual assault among adolescents*. Lexington, MA: Lexington Books.

Aizenman, M., and Kelley, G. (1988). The incidence of violence and acquaintance rape in dating relationships among college men and women. *Journal of College Student Development, 29,* 305–11.

American Association for Protecting Children. (1986). Highlights of official child neglect and abuse reporting, 1986. Denver: American Humane Association.

American Humane Association (1986). Definitions of national study data items and response categories. In *Technical Report 3*, American Humane Association.

Apter, S. J., and Propper, C. A. (1986). Ecological perspectives on youth violence. In S. J. Apter and A. P. Goldstein, *Youth violence program and prospects* (pp. 140–59). New York: Pergamon.

Arcus, M. (1986). Should family life education be required for high school students?: An examination of the issues. Family *Relations, 35*(3), 347–56.

Badgley, R. F., Allard, H. A., McCormick, N., Proudfoot, P., Fortin, D., Ogilvie, D., Rae-Grant, Q., Gelinas, P., Pepin, L., and Sutherland, S. (1984). *Sexual offenses against children* (Vol. 1). Ottawa, Canada: Minister of Supply and Services Canada.

Bandura, A. (Ed.). (1977). *Social learning theory*. Englewood Cliffs, NJ: Prentice-Hall.

Barnard, G. W., Fuller, A, K., Robbins, L., and Shaw, T. (1989). *The child molester: An integrated approach to evaluation and treatment*. New York: Brunner/Mazel.

Barth, R. P. (1988a). *Enhancing pregnancy prevention skills*. Santa Cruz, CA: Network Publications.

———. (1988b). *On their own: The experiences of youth after foster care*. School of Social Welfare, University of California at Berkeley.

———. (in press). Promoting self-protection and self-control through life skill training. In J. Poertner (Ed.). *Life skills training to prevent child abuse.* Beverly Hills, Sage.

Barth, R. P., Hacking, S., and Ash, J. R. (1986). Identifying, screening and engaging high risk clients in private non-profit child abuse prevention programs. *Child Abuse and Neglect, 16,* 99–109.

Barth, R., Middleton, K., and Wagman, E. (1989). A skill building approach to preventing teenage pregnancy. *Theory into practice, 28,* 183–190.

Bavolek, S. J. (1988). *Nurturing programs for parents and adolescents.* San Claire, WI: Human Development Resources.

Becker, J. V., Cunningham-Rathner, J., and Kaplan, M. (1986). The adolescent sexual offender. Demographics, criminal history, victims, sexual behavior and recommendations for reducing future offenses. *Journal of Interpersonal Violence, 1,* 431.

Beland, K., and Bak, K. (1986). *Talking about touching II: Personal safety for preschoolers.* Seattle: Committee for Children.

Bell, R. G. and Harper, L. V. (1977). *Child effects on adults.* Hillsdale, NJ: Lawrence Erlbaum.

Bell, R. Q., and Harper, L. V. (1977). *Child effects on adults.* Hillsdale, NJ: Lawrence Erlbaum.

Berdie, J., Berdie, M., Wexler, S. and Fisher, B. (1983). *An empirical study of families involved in adolescent maltreatment.* San Francisco: USRA Institute.

Berdie, J., Berdie, M., Wexler, S., & Fisher, B. (1983). *An empirical study of families involved in adolescent maltreatment.* San Francisco, CA: URSA.

Berlin, I. N. (1962). Mental health consultation in schools as a means of communicating mental health principles. *Journal of the American Academy of Child Psychiatry, 1,* 671–79.

Bernard, B. (1989). Life Skills for Children and Youth. Paper presented at the Texas Children's Trust Fund Forum II, January 27.

Berrick, J. D. (1988). Parental involvement in child abuse prevention training. *Child Abuse and Neglect, 12,* 543–54.

Berrick, J. D., and Gilbert, N. (in press). *The sexual abuse prevention movement.* New York: Guilford.

Besharov, B. J. (1987). Contending with overblown expectations. *Public Welfare, 45*(10), 7–11.

Binder, R., and McNeil, D. (1987). Evaluation of a school-based sexual abuse prevention program: Cognitive and emotional effects. *Child Abuse and Neglect, 11,* 497–506.

Blum, R. W., and Runyan, C. (1980). Adolescent abuse: Dimensions of the problem. *Journal of Adolescent Health Care, 1,* 121–26.

Borden, L. A., Karr, S. K., and Caldwell-Colbert, A. T. (1988). Effects of a university rape prevention program on attitudes and empathy towards rape. *Journal of College Student Development, 29,* 132–36.

Borkin, J., and Frank, L. (1986). Sexual abuse prevention for preschoolers: A pilot program. *Child Welfare, 65*(1), 75–82.

Botvin, G. J. (1986). Substance abuse prevention research: Recent developments and future directions. *Journal of School Health, 56*(9), 369–74.

Briere, J., and Runtz, M. (1989). University males' sexual interest in children: Predicting potential incidences of "pedophilia" in a conforensic sample. *Child Abuse and Neglect, 13,* 65–75.

Brim, 0., and Kagan, J. (Eds.). (1980). *Constancy and change in human development.* Cambridge, MA: Harvard University Press.

Brindis, C., Barth, R. P., and Loomis, A. (1987). Continuous counseling: Case management with teenage parents. *Social Casework, 68,* 164–72.

Brindis, C. D., and Jeremy, R. J. (1989). *Adolescent pregnancy and parenting in California: A strategic plan for action.* San Francisco: Sutter Publications.

Bronfenbrenner, U. (1977). Toward an experimental ecology of human development, *American Psychologist, 32,* 513–31.

Budin, L. E., and Johnson, C. F. (1989). Sex abuse prevention programs: Offenders' attitude about their efficacy. *Child Abuse and Neglect, 13,* 77–87.

California State Department of Education. (1989). *Model curriculum guide. Drug and alcohol abuse prevention education, AIDS prevention and control.* Sacramento, CA: Author.

Carlson, M., Muehlenhard, C., and Julsonnet, S. (1988, March). *Sexual assertiveness: Increasing women's skills in refusing unwanted sexual advances.* Paper presented at the Western Region Meeting of the Society for the Scientific Study of Sex. Dallas, TX.

Carlson, M. I., Muehlenhard, C. L., and Julsonnet, S. (1988). *Sexual assertiveness: Increasing women's skills in refusing unwanted sexual advances.* Paper presented at the Western Region meeting of the Society for the Scientific Study of Sex, Dallas, TX, March.

Chavkin, F. (1985). School social work practice: A reappraisal. *Social Work in Education, 8,* 3–13.

Children's Self-Help Project. (1983). *Elementary school curriculum.* Available from the author at 170 Fell Street, San Francisco, CA 94102.

Clarke, J. H., MacPherson, D. R., Holmes, D.R., and Jones, R. (1986). Reducing adolescent smoking: A comparison of peer-led, teacher-led, and expert-led interventions. *Journal of School Health, 56*(3), 102–6.

Cleary, P. D., Hitchcock, J. L., Semmer, N., Flinchbaugh, L. J., and Pinney, J. M. (1988). Adolescent smoking: Research and health policy. *The Millbank Quarterly, 66,* 137–71.

Cohen, J. (1977). *Statistical power analysis for the behavioral sciences* (rev. ed.). New York: Academic Press.

Comer, J. P. (1988). Educating poor minority children. *Scientific American, 259*(5), 42–48.

Committee for Children. (1989). *Second step: A violence prevention curriculum.* Seattle, WA: Committee for Children.

Conrad, D., and Hedin, D. (1982). Experiential education evaluation project. St. Paul: University of Minnesota.

Conte, J. R., and Berliner, L. (1981). Sexual abuse of children: Implications for practice. *Social Casework, 62,* 601–6.

Conte, J. R., Rosen, C., Saperstein, L., and Shermack, R. (1985). An evaluation of a program to prevent the sexual victimization of young children. *Child Abuse and Neglect, 9,* 319–28.

Conte, J. R., and Schuerman, J. R. (1987). Factors associated with an increased impact of child sexual abuse. *Child Abuse and Neglect, 11,* 202–11.

Cooke, G., and Wallace, H. (1984). The California statewide family health education and training program 1981–1982. *Journal of School Health, 54*(3), 118–21.

Cotterill, A. M. (1988). The geographic distribution of child abuse in an inner-city borough. *Child Abuse and Neglect, 12,* 461–67.

Daro, D. (1988). *Confronting child abuse: Research for effective program design.* New York: Free Press.

Daro, D., and Mitchel, L. (1989). *Child abuse fatalities continue to rise: The results of the 1988 annual fifty state survey.* Prepared by the National Center on Child Abuse Prevention Research.

Davis, G. E., and Leitenberg, H. (1987). Adolescent sex offenders. *Psychological Bulletin, 101,* 417–37.

Deisher, R. W., Wenet, G. A., Papenny, D. M., Clark, T. F., and Fehrenbach, P. A. (1982). Adolescent sexual offense behavior: The role of the physician. *Journal of Adolescent Health Care, 2,* 279–86.

De Young, M. (1982). *The sexual victimization of children.* Jefferson, NC: McFarland.

Ditson, J., and Shay, S. (1984). Use of a home-based microcomputer to analyze community data from reported cases of child abuse and neglect. *Child Abuse and Neglect, 8,* 503–9.

Dominguez, A. (1987). Unpublished report that summarized the first two years of the CAPTA project, written for the California Office of Child Abuse Prevention.

Downer, A. (1985). *Prevention of child sexual abuse: A trainer's manual.* Seattle: Seattle Institute for Child Advocacy Institute for Children.

Duerr, J. (1989). Social policy and child development: An illustration. Unpublished manuscript, School of Social Welfare, University of California, Berkeley.

Eckenrode, J., Munsch, J., Powers, J., and Doris, J. (1988). The nature and substantiation of official sexual abuse reports. *Child Abuse and Neglect, 12,* 311–19.

Education doesn't change behavior. (December 3, 1989). *Oakland Tribune,* pps. A1, A13.

Egeland, B., Sroufe, A., and Erickson, M. (1983). The developmental consequences of different patterns of maltreatment. *Child Abuse and Neglect, 7,*
459–69.

Evans, R. I. (1988). How can health lifestyles in adolescents be modified? Some
implications from a smoking prevention program. In D. K. Routh (Ed.),
Handbook of pediatric psychology (pp. 321–31). New York: Guilford
Press.

Farber, E., and Joseph, J. (1985). The maltreated adolescent: Patterns of physical abuse. *Child Abuse and Neglect, 9,* 201–6.

Felner, R. D., and Adan, A. M. (1988). The school transition environment
project: An ecological intervention and evaluation. In R. H. Price et al.
(Eds.), *Fourteen ounces of prevention.* Washington, DC: American Psychological Association.

Felner, R. D., Weissberg, R. P., and Adan, A. M. (1987). Long-term follow-up
of a school transition program. Unpublished manuscript.

Finkelhor, D. (1979). *Sexually victimized children.* New York: The Free Press.

————. (1984). *Child sexual abuse: New theory and research.* New York:
The Free Press.

————. (1986). *Sourcebook on child sexual abuse.* Beverly Hills: Sage.

————. (1988). Male victims of molest not likely to molest others. Paper
presented at Prevention Conference, Oakland, CA.

Fisher, J. D. (1988). Possible effects of reference group-based social influence
on AIDS-risk behavior and AIDS prevention. *American Psychologist, 43,*
914–920.

Flarity-White, L. A., Piper, A. M., and Muehlenhard, C. L. (1988). *Construction and validation of a videotaped role-play test measuring women's ability to refuse unwanted sexual intercourse.* Paper presented at the Western
Region meeting of the Society for the Scientific Study of Sex, Dallas TX,
March.

Fontana, V. J., and Alfaro, J. D. (1987). *High risk factors associated with child
maltreatment fatalities.* New York: Mayor's Task Force on Child Abuse
and Neglect.

Forman, S. G., and Neal, J. A. (1987). School-based substance abuse prevention programs. *Special Services in the Schools, 3*(3/4), 89–102.

Fraser, M. W., Pecora, P. J., and Haapala, D. A. (1988). *Families in Crisis.*
New York: Aldine de Gruyter.

Friedman, M. (1968). Magnitude of experimental effect and a table for its
rapid estimation. *Psychological Bulletin, 70,* 245–51.

Fryer, G., Kraizer, S., and Miyoshi, T. (1987a). Measuring actual reduction of
risk to child abuse: A new approach. *Child Abuse and Neglect, 11*(2),
173–79.

————. (1987b). Measuring children's retention of skills to resist stranger
abduction: Use of the simulation technique. *Child Abuse and Neglect,
11*(2), 181–85.

Garbarino, J. (1976). A preliminary study of some ecological correlates of child abuse: The impact of socioeconomic stress on mothers. *Child Development, 47*, 178–85.

———. (1981). Child abuse and juvenile delinquency. In R. H. Hunner and Y. E. Walker (Eds.), *Exploring the relationship between child abuse and delinquency*. Montclair, NJ: Allanheld, Osmun.

———. (1986). Can we measure success in preventing child abuse? Issues in policy, programming and research. *Child Abuse and Neglect, 10*, 143–56.

———. (1988). President's message: But are we really preventing child abuse? *Division of Child, Youth and Family Services Newsletter*, APA, *11*, No. 4, 3.

Garbarino, J., and Crouter, A. (1978). Defining the community context of parent-child relationships: The correlates of child maltreatment. *Child Development, 49*, 604–16.

Garbarino, J., and Gillian, G. (1980). *Understanding abusive families*. Lexington, MA: Lexington Books.

Garbarino, J., Guttmann, E., and Seeley, J. W. (1986). *The psychologically battered child*. San Francisco: Jossey-Bass.

Garbarino, J., Schellenbach, C. J., and Sebes, J. (1986). *Troubled youth, troubled families: Understanding families at risk for adolescent maltreatment*. New York: Adline.

Garbarino, J., and Sherman, D. (1980). Identifying high-risk neighborhoods. In J. Garbarino & S. H. Stocking (Eds.), *Protecting children from abuse and neglect: Developing and maintaining effective support systems for families* (pp. 94–108). San Francisco: Jossey-Bass.

Gil, D. (1970). *Violence against children: Physical abuse in the United States*. Cambridge, MA: Harvard University Press.

Gilbert, N., Daro, D., Duerr, J., Prohn N. L., and Nyman, N. (1988). Child sexual abuse prevention: Evaluation of educational materials for pre-school programs. Unpublished manuscript, University of California at Berkeley.

Gilbert, N., Duerr-Berrick, J., LeProhn, N., and Nyman, N. (1989). *Protecting young children from sexual abuse: Does preschool training work?* Lexington, MA: Lexington Books.

Giovannoni, J., and Billingsley, A. (1970). Child neglect among the poor: A study of parental adequacy in families of three ethnic groups. *Child Welfare, 49*, 196–204.

Goodstadt, M. S. (1987). Prevention strategies for drug abuse. *Issues in Science and Technology, 3*(2), 28–35.

Gordon, L. (1988). *Heroes of their own lives: The politics and history of family violence: Boston, 1880–1960*. New York: Viking Press.

Gore, D. (1987). Parent/school collaboration project. Unpublished manuscript, Milwaukee Public Schools, Milwaukee, WI.

Gottesman, S. T. (1977). Police attitudes toward rape before and after a training program. *Journal of Psychiatric Nursing and Mental Health Services, 15*, 14–18.

Gough, D. (1988). Approaches to child abuse prevention. In *Early prediction and prevention of child abuse* (pp. 107–120). New York: John Wiley and Sons.

Groth, A. N. (1978). Patterns of sexual assault against children and adolescents. In A. Burgess, A. N. Groth, L. L. Holmstrum, and S. M. Sgroi (Eds.), *Sexual assault of children and adolescents.* Lexington, MA: Lexington Books.

Guerney, L. (1986). Prospects for intervention with troubled youth and troubled families. In J. Garbarino, C. J. Schellenbach, and J. M. Sebes (Eds.), *Troubled youth, troubled families* (pp. 255–92). New York: Aldine de Gruyter.

Guerney, L., and Moore, L. (1983). Phone friend: A prevention-oriented service for latchkey children. *Children Today, 12*(4), 5–10.

Hall, J. A. (1984). Empirically based treatment for parent-adolescent conflict. *Social Casework, 65,* 487–95.

Hall, R. P., and Kassees, J. M. (1989). Adolescent sexual abuse prevention project. Paper presented at Eighth National Conference on Child Abuse and Neglect, Salt Lake City, UT, October 23–25.

Hamilton, S. F., and Fenzel, L. M. (1988). The impact of volunteer experience on adolescent social development: Evidence of program effects. *Journal of Adolescent Research, 3,*(3), 123–132.

Hampton, R., and Newberger, E. (1985). Child abuse incidents and reporting by hospitals: Significance of severity, class, and race. *American Journal of Public Health, 75,* 56–60.

Harrison, C. H. (1987). *Student service, the new Carnegie unit.* Lawrenceville, NJ: Princeton University Press.

Harvey, P., Forehand, R., Brown, C., and Holmes, T. (1988). The prevention of sexual abuse: Examination of the effectiveness of a program with kindergarten-age children. *Behavior Therapy, 19,* 429–35.

Haugaard, J. J. (1987). The consequences of child sexual abuse: A college survey. Unpublished manuscript, Department of Psychology, University of Virginia, Charlottesville.

Hawkins, J. D., Lishner, D. M., Catalano, R. F., and Howard, M. 0. (1986). Childhood predictions of adolescent substance abuse: Toward an empirically grounded theory. *Journal of Children in Contemporary Society, 8,* 11–48.

Hayes, C. D. (1987). *Risking the future: Adolescent sexuality, pregnancy, and childbearing.* Washington, DC: National Academy Press.

Herz, E. J., and Reis, J. S. (1987). Family life education for young inner-city teens: Identifying needs. *Journal of Youth and Adolescence, 16*(4), 361–77.

Hughes, J., and Sandler, B. (1987). *Friends raping friends: Could it happen to you?* Washington, DC: Project on the Status and Education of Women, Association of American Colleges.

Jayaratne S. (1977). Child abusers as parents and children: A review. *Social Work, 22,* 5–7.

Jewell, D. L. (1989). *Confronting child abuse through recreation.* Springfield, IL: Charles Thomas.

Joseph P. Kennedy Foundation. (1988). A community of caring: Teachers' guide. Washington, DC: Author.

Joseph P. Kennedy Foundation. (1988). *Community of caring background information.* Washington, D.C.: Author.

Kadushin, A. K., and Martin, J. A. (1981). *Child abuse: An interactional event.* New York: Columbia University Press.

Kaufman, J., and Zigler, E. (1987). Do abused children become abusive parents? *American Journal of Orthopsychiatry, 57*(2), 186–92.

Kean, T. H. (1989). The life you save may be your own: New Jersey addresses Prevention of Adolescent Problems. *American Psychologist, 44,* 828–30.

Kenney, A. M., Guardado, S., and Brown, L. (1989). Sex education and AIDS education in the schools: What states and large school districts are doing. *Family Planning Perspectives, 21,* 56–64.

Killan, J. D. (1985). Prevention of adolescent tobacco smoking: The social pressure resistance training approach. *Journal of Child Psychology and Psychiatry, 26*(1), 7–15.

Kinney, J., Haapala, D. Booth, C., and Leavitt, S. (1988). The homebuilders model. In J. Whittaker et al. (Eds.), *Improving practice technology for work with high risk families* (pp. 37–68). Seattle: University of Washington.

Kirby, D. (1984). *Sexuality education: An evaluation of programs and their effectiveness.* Santa Cruz, CA: Network Publications.

Kleemeier, C., Webb, C., Hazzard, A., and Pohl, J. (1988). Child sexual abuse prevention training model. *Child Abuse and Neglect, 12,* 255–62.

Kolko, D. J. (1988). Educational programs to promote awareness and prevention of child sexual victimization: A review and methodological critique. *Clinical Psychology Review, 8,* 195–209.

Kolko, D. J., Moser, J. T., and Hughes, J. (1989). Classroom teaching in sexual victimization awareness and prevention skills: An extension of the Red Flag/Green Flag People Program. *Journal of Family Violence, 4*(1), 25–45.

Korbin, J. (1980). The cultural context of child abuse and neglect. *Child Abuse and Neglect, 4,* 3–13.

Koss, M. P., Dinero, T. E., and Seibel, C. A. (1988). Stranger and acquaintance rape: Are there differences in the victim's experience? *Psychology of Women Quarterly, 12,* 1–24.

Koss, M. P., and Oros, C. J. (1982). Sexual experiences survey: A research instrument investigating sexual aggression and victimization. *Journal of Consulting and Clinical Psychology, 50,* 455–57.

Kosta, S. L., and Moore, C. (1989). Positive parenting—A curriculum for the prevention of child abuse and neglect. Paper presented at eighth National Conference on Child Abuse and Neglect, Salt Lake City, UT, October 23–25.

Kraizer, S. K. (1986). Rethinking prevention. *Child Abuse and Neglect, 10,* 259–61.

Kraizer, S. K., and Fryer, G. E. (1988). Preventing child sexual abuse: Measuring actual behavioral change attributable to a school-based curriculum. Unpublished manuscript. Palisades, NY: Health Education Systems.

Kraizer, S., Witte, S., and Fryer, G. (1989). Child sexual abuse prevention programs: What makes them effective in protecting children? *Children Today,* Sept.–Oct., 23–27.

Kraus, R. G. (1984). *Recreational leisure in modern society.* Glenview, IL: Scott Foresman.

Krugman, R. D. (1988). It's time to wave the yellow flag. *Child Abuse and Neglect, 12,* 293–94.

Larrabee, M. J., and Wilson, B. D. (1981). Teaching teenagers to cope through family life situations. *The School Counselor, 11,* 117–23.

Lefkowitz, B. (1987). *Tough change: Growing up on your own in America.* New York: Free Press.

Lehman, N., and Krupp, S. L. (1984). Incidence of alcohol-related domestic violence: An assessment. *Alcohol Health and Research World,* 8(2), 23–27.

Levanthal, J. M. (1987). Programs to prevent sexual abuse: What outcomes should be measured? *Child Abuse and Neglect, 11,* 169–71.

Levy, B. (1984). *Skills for violence-free relationships: Curriculum for young people ages 13–18.* California: Southern California Coalition on Battered Women.

Libbee, P., and Bybee, R. (1979). The physical abuse of adolescents. *Journal of Social Issues, 35,* 101–26.

Liddell, T., Young, B., and Yamagishi, M. (1988). Implementation and evaluation of a preschool sexual abuse prevention resource. Unpublished manuscript. Seattle Department of Human Resources, Seattle, WA.

Lindholm, K. J., and Willey, R. (1986). Ethnic differences in child abuse and sexual abuse. *Hispanic Journal of Behavioral Sciences,* 8(2), 111–25.

Long, T. J., and Long, L. (1988). Hotlines for children: What makes them effective? *Children Today,* 17(2), 22–25.

Longo, R. E., and Groth, A. N. (1983). Juvenile sex offenses in the history of adult rapist and child molesters. *International Journal of Offender Therapy and Comparative Criminology, 27,* 150–55.

Longo, R., and McFadin, B. (1981). Sexually inappropriate behavior—Development of the sexual offender. *Law and Order, 29,* 21–23.

Lourie, I. (1977). The phenomenon of the abused adolescent: A clinical study. *Victimology, 2,* 268–76.

Lourie, I. S. (1979). Family dynamics and the abuse of adolescents: A case for a developmental phase specific model of child abuse. *Child Abuse and Neglect, 3,* 967–74.

Marion, M. (1982). Primary prevention of child abuse: The role of the family life educator. *Family Relations,* 31(4), 575–82.

Mayer, G. R., Butterworth, T., Nafpaktitis, M., and Sulzer-Azaroff, B. (1983). Preventing school vandalism and improving discipline: A three-year study. *Journal of Applied Behavior Analysis, 16,* 355–369.

Miller-Perrin, L. L., and Wurtele, S. K. (1986). Harmful effect of school-based sexual abuse prevention programs. Paper presented at the American Psychological Association Convention, Washington, DC, August 12.

Millstein, S. G. (1988). *The potential of school-linked centers to promote adolescent health and development.* New York: Carnegie Council on Adolescent Development.

Mitnick, M. (1989). Sexual health and responsibility program: Preventing adolescents from becoming perpetrators. Paper presented at eighth National Conference on Child Abuse and Neglect, Salt Lake City, UT, October 23–25.

Moskowitz, J. M. (1989). The primary prevention of alcohol problems: A critical review of the research literature. *Journal of Studies on Alcohol, 50,* 54–88.

Muehlenhard, C. L., Friedman, D. E., and Thomas, C. M. (1985). Is date rape justifiable? The effects of dating activity: Who initiated, who paid, and men's attitudes towards women. *Psychology of Women Quarterly, 9*(3), 297–310.

Muehlenhard, C. L., and Linton, M. A. (1987). Date rape and sexual aggression in dating situations: Incidence and risk factors. *Journal of Counseling Psychology, 34*(2), 186–96.

National Center on Child Abuse and Neglect. (1981). *National incidence study of child abuse and neglect.* Washington, D.C.: U.S. GPO.

———. (1986). *Executive summary: The national study of the incidence and severity of child abuse and neglect.* DHHS Publication No. OHDS 81-30329. Washington, DC: U.S. Government Printing Office.

Nelson, B. J. (1985). *Making an issue of child abuse.* Chicago: University of Chicago Press.

Nelson, M., and Clark, K. (1986). *The educator's guide to preventing child sexual abuse.* Santa Cruz, CA: Network Publications.

Network against Teenage Violence. (1987). *When love really hurts: Dating violence curriculum.* Williston, ND: Family Crisis Shelter.

New York State Council on Children and Families. (1988). *State of the child.* New York: Author.

Olds, D. L. (1981). The Prenatal/Early infancy project. In R. H. Price, E. L. Cowen, R. P. Lorion, and J. Ramos-McKay (Eds.), *fourteen ounces of prevention.* Washington, DC: American Psychological Association.

———. (1988). The prenatal/early infancy project. In R. H. Price, E. L. Cowen, R. P. Lorion, and Ramos-McKay. (Eds.). *14 ounces of prevention: A casebook for practitioners* (pp. 9–23). Washington, D.C.: American Psychological Association.

Olds, D., Chamberlin, R., and Tatlebaum, R. (1986). Preventing child abuse and neglect: A randomized trial of nurse home visitation. *Pediatrics, 78,* 65–78.

Olson, L., and Holmes W. (1983). Youth at risk: Adolescents and maltreatment. Boston: Center for Applied Social Research.

Osgood, D. W., Johnston, L. D., O'Malley, P. M., and Bachman, J. G. (1988). The generality of deviance in late adolescence and early adulthood. *American Sociological Review, 53,* 81–93.

Patterson, G. R., Dishion, T. J., and Bank, L. (1984). Family interaction: A process model of deviancy training. In L. Eron (Ed.), special edition of *Aggressive Behavior, 10,* 253–67.

Pavelec, M. B. (1989). The Parent linking project: A school-based child abuse prevention program for teenage parents. Paper presented at eighth National Conference on Child Abuse and Neglect, Salt Lake City, UT, October 23–25.

Pelcovitz, D., Kaplan, S., Samit, C. Krieger, R, and Cornelius, P. (1984). Adolescent abuse: Family structure and implication for treatment. *Journal of Child Psychiatry, 23,* 85–90.

Pelton, L. H. (1978). Child abuse and neglect: The myth of classlessness. *American Journal of Orthopsychiatry, 48,* 608–17.

Pelton, L. H. (Ed.). (1981). *The social context of child abuse and neglect.* New York: Human Sciences Press.

Pennekamp, M., and Freeman, E. M. (1988). Toward a partnership perspective: Schools, families, and school social workers. *Social Work In Education, 10*(4) 246–59

Perry, C. L., Telch, M. J., Killen, J., and Dass, R., (1983). High school smoking prevention: The relative efficacy of varied treatments and instructors. *Adolescence, 18*(71), 561–66.

Pierce, L. H., and Pierce, R. L. (1984). Race as a factor in the sexual abuse of children. *Social Work Research and Abstracts, 20*(1), 9–14.

Plummer, C. (1984). Preventing sexual abuse: What in-school programs teach children. Unpublished manuscript. Prevention Training Associates, P.0. Box 421, Kalamazoo, MI, 49005.

Plummer, K. (1981). Pedophilia: Constructing a sociological baseline. In M. Cook and K. Howells (Eds.), *Adult sexual interest in children.* London: Academic.

Poche, C., Bouwer, R., and Swearingen, M. (1981). Teaching self-protection to young children. *Journal of Applied Behavioral Analysis, 14,* 169–75.

Poche, C., Yoder, P., and Miltenberger, R. (1988). Teaching self-protection to children using television techniques. *Journal of Applied Behavior Analysis, 21,* 253–261.

Powers, J. P., and Eckenrode, J. (1988). The maltreatment of adolescents. *Child Abuse and Neglect, 12,* 189–99.

Price, R. H., Cowen, E. L., Lorion, R. P., and Ramos-McKay, J. (1988). Model prevention programs: Epilogue and future prospects. In R. H. Price, E. L.

Cowen, R. P. Lorion, and J. Ramos-McKay (Eds.), *fourteen ounces of prevention*. Washington, DC: American Psychological Association.

Proctor, S. E. (1986). A developmental approach to pregnancy prevention with early adolescent females. *Journal of School Health*, *56*(8), 313–16.

Randazzo, J. (1989). Sexual assault by the male adolescent offender. Unpublished manuscript, School of Social Welfare, University of California at Berkeley.

Ray, J. (1984). Evaluation of the child sex abuse evaluation project. Paper presented at the Second National Conference for Family Violence Researchers, Durham, NH, March 27.

Reppucci, N. D. (1987). Prevention and ecology: Teen-age pregnancy, child sexual abuse, and organized youth sports. *American Journal of Community Psychology*, *15*(1), 1–22.

Reppucci, N. D., and Haugaard, J. J. (1989). Prevention of child sexual abuse: Myth or reality. *American Psychologist*, *44*(10), 1266–75.

Resnick, H. (1983). *Saying no programs*. Prevention Branch, Division of Prevention and Communications, National Institute on Drug Abuse. (Under Contract No. 271-81-4907), Feb. 1–13.

Rosenthal, J. A. (1988). Patterns of reported child abuse and neglect. *Child Abuse and Neglect*, *12*, 263–71.

Russell, D. E. H. (1983). The incidence and prevalence of intrafamilial and extrafamilial sexual abuse of female children. *Child Abuse and Neglect*, *7*, 133.

———. (1986). *The secret trauma: Incest in the lives of girls and women*. New York: Basic Books.

———. (1984). *Sexual exploitation: Rape, child sexual abuse and sexual harassment*. Beverly Hills: Sage.

Rutter, M. (1979). Protective factors in children's responses to stress and disadvantage. In M. W. Kent and J. E. Rolf (Eds.), *Primary prevention of psychopathology: Social competence in children*, Vol. 3. Hanover, NH: University Press of New England.

Sancilio, F. M. (1987). Peer interaction as a method of therapeutic interaction with children. *Clinical Psychology Review*, *7*, 475–500.

Sandoval, J., Davis, J. M., and Wilson, M. P. (1987). An overview of the school-based prevention of adolescent suicide. *Special Services on the Schools*, *3* (3/4), 103–20.

Schillenbach, C. J., and Guerney, L. F. (1987). Identification of adolescent abuse and future intervention prospects. *Journal of Adolescence*, *10*, 1–10.

Schinke, S. P., Blythe, B. J., and Gilchrist, L. D. (1981). Cognitive and behavioral prevention of adolescent pregnancy. *Journal of Counseling Psychology*, *28*, 451–54.

Schinke, S. P., and Gilchrist, L. D. (1985). Preventing substance abuse with children and adolescents. *Journal of Consulting and Clinical Psychology*, *53*(5), 596–602.

Schultz, J. B., and Adams, D. U. (1987). Family life education needs of mentally disabled adolescents. *Adolescence*, *85*, 221–30.

Seager, L. (1986). Personal communication with the Office of Child Abuse Prevention, Sacramento, CA.

Sedney, M. A., and Brooks, B. (1984). Factors associated with a history of childhood sexual experiences in a non-clinical female population. *Journal of the American Academy of Child Psychiatry, 23*, 215–18.

Seitz, V., Rosenbaum, L., and Apfel, N. (1985). Effects of family support intervention: A ten year follow-up. *Child Development, 56*, 376–91.

Severson, H. H. (1984). Adolescent social drug use: School prevention program. *School Psychology Review, 13*(2), 150–61.

Shunk, D. H. (1987). Peer models and children's behavioral change. *Review of Educational Research, 57*(2), 149–74.

Sigurdson, E., Doig, T., and Strang, M. (1985). What do children know about preventing sexual assault: How can their awareness be increased? Paper presented at the seventy-seventh Annual Conference of the Canadian Public Health Association, Vancouver, BC, May.

Smith, H., and Israel, E. (1987). Sibling incest: A study of the dynamics of 25 cases. *Child Abuse and Neglect, 11*, 101–8.

Snow, W. H., Gilchrist, L. D., and Schinke, S. P. (1985). A critique of progress in adolescent smoking prevention. *Children and Youth Services Review, 7*, 1–20.

Solomon, M. Z., and DeJong, W. (1986). Recent sexually transmitted disease prevention efforts and their implications for AIDS health education. *Health Education Quarterly, 13*(4), 301–15.

Sourcebook of Criminal Justice Statistics. (1988). Washington, DC: Bureau of Justice and Statistics.

Spearly, J. L., and Lauderdale, M. (1983). Community characteristics and ethnicity in the prediction of child maltreatment rates. *Child Abuse and Neglect, 7*, 91–105.

State of California, Assembly Bill 2443. (1984). Chapter 1638: Maxine Waters Child Abuse Prevention Training Act. Sacramento, CA: Author.

Starn, J. R., and Paperny, D. M. (1986). Computer-assisted instruction to avert teen pregnancy. Paper presented at the Annual Meeting of the American Public Health Association, Las Vegas, September.

Stets, J. E., and Pirog-Good, M. A. (1989). Patterns of physical and sexual abuse for men and women in dating relationships: A descriptive analysis. *Journal of Family Violence, 4*(1), 63–77.

Stilwell, S. L., Lutzker, J. R., and Greene, B. F. (1988). Evaluation of a sexual abuse prevention program for preschoolers. *Journal of Family Violence, 13*(4), 269–81.

Stout, J. W., and Rivara, F. P. (1989). Schools and sex education: Does it work? *Pediatrics, 83*, 375–79.

Swan, H., Press, A., and Briggs, (1985). Child sexual abuse prevention: Does it work? *Child Welfare, 64*, 395–405.

Testa, M., and Lawlor, E. (1985). *Report: 1985 the state of the child in Illinois: A Chaplin Hall report*. Chicago: University of Chicago.

Tharinger, D. J., Krivacdka, J. J., Laye-McDonough, Jamison, L., Vincent, G., and Hedlund, A. (1988). Prevention of child sexual abuse: An analysis of issues, educational programs, and research findings. *School Psychology Review*, 17(4), 614–34.

Tisdelle, D. A., and St. Lawrence, J. S. (1986). Interpersonal problem-solving competency: Review and critique of the literature. *Clinical Psychology Review*, 6, 337–56.

Tobler, N. S. (1986). Meta-analysis of 143 adolescent drug prevention programs: Quantitative outcome results of program participants compared to a control or comparison group. *Journal of Drug Issues*, 16(4), 537–67.

U.S. Department of Justice. (1983). *Uniform crime report*. Federal Bureau of Investigation. Washington, D.C.: U.S. Department of Printing.

———. (1986). *Child abuse: Prelude to delinquency?* Washington, DC: Office of Juvenile Justice and Delinquency Prevention.

Valentine-Dunham, K., and Gipson, M. T. (1980). A brief preventative approach to child abuse. Presented at the meeting of the Association for the Advancement of Behavior Therapy, November.

Wald, M. (1988). Family preservations: Are we moving too fast? *Public Health*, 46, 33–38.

Waller, A. E., Baker, S. P., and Szocka, A. (1989). Childhood injury deaths: National analysis and geographic variations. *American Journal of Public Health*, 79, 310–315.

Waterman, J., and Lusk, R. (1986). Scope of the problem. In K. MacFarlane, J. Waterman, S. Conerly, L. Damon, M. Durfee and S. Long (Eds.), *Sexual abuse of young children* (pp. 3–12). New York: The Guilford Press.

Westat Associates. (1981). National study of the incidence and severity of child abuse and neglect. Prepared for the National Center on Child Abuse and Neglect.

Wexler, S. (1989). Reports of child sexual abuse: Discrepancies and responses. Unpublished doctoral dissertation, University of California at Berkeley.

White, B. L. (1980). Primary prevention: Beginning at the begining. *Personnel and Guidance Journal*, 58, 338–43.

———. (1986). Primary prevention: Beginning at the begining. *Personnel and Guidance Journal*, 58, 1–13.

White, M., and Nichols, D. D. (1981). *Assault and rape awareness: Using data and task forces to respond to a community college concern* (Report no. SC 820 316). Oakland, MI: Oakland Community College. (ERIC Document Reproduction Service No. ED 317 940).

Widom, C. S. (1989). Child abuse, neglect, and adult behavior: Research design and findings on criminality, violence, and child abuse. *American Journal of Orthopsychiatry*, 59(3), 355–67.

William T. Grant Foundation. (1988). *Report of Commission on Work, Family, and Citizenship*. New York: Author.

Williams, R., Ward, D., and Gray, L. (1985). The persistence of experimentally inducted cognitive change: A neglected dimension in the assessment of drug prevention programs. *Journal of Drug Education*, 15, 33–42.

Wolf, F. M. (1986). *Meta analysis: Quantitative methods for research synthesis.* California: Sage Publications, Inc.

Wurtele, S. K., Marrs, S. R., and Miller-Perrin, C. L. (1987). Practice makes perfect? The role of participant modeling in sexual abusive prevention programs. *Journal of Consulting and Clinical Psychology, 55,* 599–602.

Wurtele, S., Saslawsky, D., Miller, C., Marrs, S., and Britcher, J. (1986). *Teaching personal safety skills for potential prevention of sexual abuse: A comparison of treatments.* Pullman, WA: Department of Psychology, Washington State University.

Wyatt, G. E. (1985). The sexual abuse of Afro-American and White-American women in childhood. *Child Abuse and Neglect, 9,* 507–19.

Zambrana, R. E., and Aguirre-Molina, M. (1987). Alcohol abuse prevention among Latino adolescents: A strategy for intervention. *Journal of Youth and Adolescence, 16*(2), 97–113.

Zuravin, S. J., and Taylor, R. (1987). The ecology of child maltreatment: Identifying and characterizing high-risk neighborhoods. *Child Welfare, 66,* 497–506.

Index

About the Authors

Richard P. Barth, M.S.W., Ph.D., is associate professor, School of Social Welfare, University of California, associate director of the Family Welfare Research Group and chairman of the School Social Work Program. He was the principal investigator of the High School Child Abuse Prevention Evaluation Project. Professor Barth teaches graduate courses in child welfare research, policy, and practice. He is an editor of *Children and Youth Services Review,* the *Journal of Adolescent Research,* and *Social Work In Education.* He is the author of *Social and Cognitive Treatment of Children and Adolescents* (Jossey-Bass 1986), *Adoption and Disruption* (Aldine 1988), *Enhancing Pregnancy Prevention Skills* (Network Publications 1989), and more than sixty articles in major children's services and research journals. He has authored and evaluated several life-skills training programs. He has also completed research on perinatal child abuse prevention services, outcomes of permanency planning projects, interagency services for seriously emotionally disturbed children, services to teenage parents, independent living programs for adolescents leaving foster care, family preservation services, child welfare training, and school-based pregnancy prevention programs. He is the winner of the University of Chicago's Frank Bruel Prize for excellence in child welfare scholarship and a Fulbright scholar.

David S. Derezotes, L.C.S.W., Ph.D., was project director of the High School Child Abuse Prevention Evaluation Project. Professor Derezotes has had over ten years of clinical experience in the area of child abuse treatment and prevention. He has provided psychotherapy to abused children and adolescents and

their families, as well as with abusive parents and other offenders at a variety of service locations. Professor Derezotes has
helped develop and facilitate parenting classes for court-referred
abusive and high-risk parents through several programs in San
Diego. He has also led groups for adults molested as children,
preadoptive parents, and intergenerational families at a variety of
settings. Professor Derezotes has taught child abuse training
classes for professionals at three universities. His professional
experience also includes hospice social work, protective services
social work, and special education. He is now assistant professor
of social work, University of Utah, and in private practice in Salt
Lake City.